TENTS

W9-BCF-751

TORVALD FAEGRE has spent the past few years
gathering the material for this book. He has
drawn the illustrations for three yurt plans published by William Coperthwaite, and has constructed his own yurt in which he lived in Wis-
consin and New Hampshire. He is a carpenter,
currently rehabilitating old buildings in Chicago.

TENTS

ARCHITECTURE OF THE NOMADS

TORVALD FAEGRE

Illustrated by the Author

ANCHOR BOOKS

ANCHOR PRESS/DOUBLEDAY GARDEN CITY, NEW YORK 1979

FERNALD LIBRARY
COLBY-SAWYER COLLEGE
NEW LONDON, N.H. 0325

GN
414.3
T45
F33

11/79 5.36

77310

ACKNOWLEDGMENTS

To my mother who initiated my interest in tents by raising me
in one in my first year;
to my father who suggested the idea for this book;
to my brother Aron for critical advice;
to Simone Collier for support and help with the typing;
to Nancy Longwell for typing the first draft;
to Barbara Ann Collier for the use of her typewriter.

The Anchor Books edition is the first publication of *Tents: Architecture of the Nomads.*

Anchor Books edition: 1979

Library of Congress Cataloging in Publication Data
Faegre, Torvald.
Tents.

Bibliography: p. 165
1. Tents.   2. Nomads.   I. Title.
GN414.3.T45F33   728

ISBN: 0-385-11656-x
Library of Congress Catalog Card Number 77–25588

Copyright © 1979 by Torvald Faegre

ALL RIGHTS RESERVED
PRINTED IN THE UNITED STATES OF AMERICA

CONTENTS

INTRODUCTION 1

CHAPTER ONE

THE BLACK TENT 9

CHAPTER TWO

THE MIDDLE EASTERN
MAT-SKIN TENT 61

CHAPTER THREE

THE YURT 79

CHAPTER FOUR

SIBERIAN TENTS 99

CHAPTER FIVE

THE LAPP TENT 115

CHAPTER SIX

THE INUIT TENT 125

CHAPTER SEVEN

TENTS OF THE
NORTH AMERICAN TAIGA   137

CHAPTER EIGHT

THE TIPI   149

SOURCES   163

BIBLIOGRAPHY   165

The very simplicity and nakedness of man's life in the primitive ages imply this advantage at least, that they left him still but a sojourner in nature. When he was refreshed with food and sleep he contemplated his journey again. He dwelt, as it were, in a tent in this world, and was either treading the valley, or crossing the plains, or climbing the mountain tops. But lo! men have become the tools of their tools.

—HENRY DAVID THOREAU

INTRODUCTION

A man's tent is like a god's temple.

—KIRGIZ PROVERB

This book is a collection of the principal tent designs of the nomads of the world. These designs form a significant part of the world's architecture but, like most vernacular architecture, have been little known or understood. My purpose is to bring together these tent designs so that they may be examined, compared, and—most important—used, for I believe these designs to be a practical architecture, even outside the environments where each tent is used. Not that the tents seen here need such justification, for no architecture can surpass them for beauty or cleverness of design. But the very qualities that are the essence of the tent—portability, lightness, and flexibility—are qualities that can be useful to a variety of design problems. These practical qualities can, and have been, applied to our own architecture to advantage. I will focus first on the tent itself as a special kind of vernacular architecture.

The tents of the nomads provide a unique look into the origins of human shelter and its subsequent evolution. Since nomads occupy the marginal areas of the world, they have been less subject to change than many settled peoples; because of their ability to move they have remained a free people. When outside forces encroached, the nomads simply rolled up their tents and moved on. Thus did the Israelites, after years of slavery in Egypt, return to the freedom of the desert and by doing so retained their Hebrew heritage. Thus did the Tuareg of North Africa move into the depths of the Sahara, avoiding first Roman and then Arab domination.

The tent is not man's earliest dwelling, for it is difficult to make a fully portable dwelling; but the simplest dwellings we know of—the windscreen and the hut—are very close to being tents. Most of the materials used for these types of shelters are easily moved so that the windscreen or the hut can quite easily be converted into a tent. In fact, it is impossible to draw a clear line between the moveable tent and the stationary hut. Many tents are only "semiportable"—that is, the frame is left in place and only the cover is moved. Many of the most sophisticated tents retain the pole frames of the primitive huts from which they evolved. In any case, it is clear that the tent reaches far into the past and provides us with a link to that past which has been lost in most sedentary dwelling.

In a sense, tents are the truest *architecture:* our word *architect* comes from the Greek *archi,* "one who directs" and *tectos,* the "weaving." The common house of ancient Greece had walls of wattle and daub—a mat of woven branches daubed with clay or mud. These wall are akin to the woven mat walls used all over the world in tents and houses, walls coated with clay or mud to windproof them. Both mat tents and black tents still use such walls today.

Tents are not only important because they reveal to us the roots of our architecture, but also because they are still useful today. Tents are being rediscovered for what they are—dwellings that are practical, inexpensive, and simple to construct. A few years ago, it looked as if the tipi was headed for extinction. Now the tipi is being used in greater and greater numbers by both Native Americans and whites. The portable yurt is being used in this country just as it is in Mongolia, with wood floors and iron stoves.

Even though this is a sedentary culture, a group of "seminomads" forsake their solid houses every summer and dwell in tents for a short time. A few campers even continue to dwell in tents year around. Unlike nomad tents, most camping tents are not designed for year-around use. Camping is not true nomadism, but both nomads and campers travel and use tents. There are several advantages to living in tents in this culture: It is possible to borrow land or squat for a while since the tent does not alter the landscape; tents can provide a way around restrictive building codes—at least for a while. Large stationary tents (pneumatic structures) are being used even in the largest cities for warehouses and tennis court covers.

It is interesting that many of the recent innovations claimed by contemporary architects have been in use by nomads for millennia. Multiple triangles fastened together in a regular pattern—the basis for the geodesic dome—are found in the tipi, in the Siberian yaranga, and the yurt. The tensile structures of the architect Frei Otto (used as pavilions for the Munich Olympics and the Montreal Expo) bear a close resemblance to the black tents of the Middle East. I do not mean to belittle the modern architect, but I believe that the nomad designer long ago worked out the possibilities inherent in the materials she had at hand. New materials and formulae will not extend the natural limits imposed on all materials, whether wool or plastic, wood or steel.

An example of a modern designer who did look to nomad design for inspiration is Bill Coperthwaite. He set out to develop an inexpensive dwelling that could be built with little skills in a minimum amount of time. He found his prototype in the Mongolian yurt. Using the key yurt elements—the circular walls, the tension band, the crown or compression ring, and the conical roof—he designed a variety of stationary yurts which have been built in many locations around the world. I am sure that other nomad designs can similarly be put to use.

This book is not meant to be a construction manual for the tents illustrated. I have tried to provide as much material as possible to aid in the actual construction of these tents, but there are gaps in the information that I could obtain. Besides, few of these designs can be built exactly as the nomads did in the past. Substitutions are in order, but any substitution may alter the very nature of the design itself. Of course, the nomads have themselves been substituting one material for another from the very beginning, and this is one of the reasons that these designs have evolved over the years. Buffalo skin was replaced by canvas in the tipi, and sealskin was replaced with sailcloth in the Inuit tupiq.

Not to be overlooked in our study of these tents is the value inherent in non-permanent building. Most nomad tents last only as long as the tent family itself. The life of the cover materials is usually short—five to ten years—so that these have to be periodically replaced, but when the tent family dies their home dies with them. Contrast this with our own buildings. Traditionally designed to last for generations, they are often torn down before they are worn out or left to fall down through neglect. Perhaps we should build less durable buildings. Frei Otto has cited the temporary nature of his structures as an advantage because, in his words, "they will not clutter up the landscape for future generations."

Is it not remarkable that the nomads, while building nonpermanent shelter, have a building tradition that is more durable than ours? The designs of the nomad tents have survived the centuries that have seen great stone monuments turn to dust. If these tents have sheltered a portion of mankind so well in the past, might they not be useful in the future?

THE NOMAD

The hoe brings shame upon the house.

—TUAREG ADAGE

The Rwala Bedouins divide mankind into the settled (*hazar*) and the nomad (*arab*), and they leave no doubt as to which way of life is superior. Nomad life is a free life, settled life is slavery. The farmer who is "tied to the soil" is just that—tied. But the nomad's freedom is at a price: He is dependent on pasture for his animals, and this pasture cannot always be depended on. There have always been droughts when the pasture withers and dies and the nomad is left with nothing. The desert demands an austerity and toughness of its people. The nomad, stamped by these conditions, has little sympathy for the soft life of the villager or city dweller. The settled peoples, in turn, have no sympathy for the nomad, who in their eyes is a parasite and a thief.

The dispute, we are told, began when Cain, the tiller of ground, slew his brother Abel, the herdsman. The Old Testament chronicles the innumerable battles that arose between villager and nomad and the conditions that forced a people to choose one way of life or the other. This conflict has never been resolved, but the biblical account makes it apparent that God, or Yahweh, sides with the nomads. This is not surprising if we know that Yahweh was originally a nomad god—the Bedouin god of flocks and herds.

The story of Abraham and his nephew Lot offers another tale of the conflict. Abraham, originally a city dweller, leaves the city and becomes a nomad. He and Lot travel to Canaan with their flocks and live as seminomads at the desert's edge. Abraham and Lot quarrel over the division of their herds. Lot leaves for the "cities of the plain" and "pitches his tent toward Sodom." We know that Lot is punished for his choice—Yahweh destroys the sinful cities and turns Lot's wife into a pillar of salt merely for looking at the destruction. But Abraham, who stayed with the pure life of the nomad, prospers and his two sons, Ishmael and Isaac, live on to father those two great nomad tribes, the Arabs and the Jews.

In spite of the conflict between nomadism and settled agriculture, they are really but two poles of a continuum. Many tribes combine both ways. The seminomad plants crops and then moves off with the herds to pasture lands and returns again at harvest time. The seminomad may live all year around in a tent or may live part of the time in a solid house, but he always considers himself first a nomad. One type of seminomad, the transhumant, may live part of the year in a tent, but has his base in settled villages and considers himself first a farmer. The transhumant is found in mountain areas where the herds are moved to highland pastures for the summer.

Actually, these categories—nomad, seminomad, transhumant—are never absolute when applied to a particular people. Some tribes have all types within their ranks, and over the course of time individual tribes have shifted categories as conditions changed. Time and time again the Old Testament recounts the famines that drove a nomadic people to take refuge among the settled. Abraham left Canaan during a famine and stayed in Egypt for a time. Many years later another famine drove his descendants into Egypt again, but this time the Hebrews stayed too long and lost their desert survival skills. They became slaves. It was Moses, who married a Bedouin woman and relearned the desert ways of the nomads, who guided them out of Pharaoh's Land and into the desert wilderness. By becoming nomadic again, the Hebrews regained their freedom.

The forms of nomadism differ widely the world over, but one condition is universally responsible for this way of life—the lack of water. Whether the land be arctic tundra, taiga forest, steppe, or desert, the lands of the nomad are dry. Much of this land cannot be cultivated without irrigation, and for this there must be a river or a well. Thus, the settled peoples are crowded together on the river banks or at the oases and use but a small fraction of the land. The rest of this arid zone was closed to man until animals that could exploit it were domesticated.

The earliest nomadism began in the Middle East and Central Asia with the domestication of the sheep and the goat. But the early farmers who kept

Rainfall: ■ less than 250 mm.
▨ more than 250 mm.

Domain of the Camel   Dromedary ▥
                       Bactrian ▨

these flocks never took them very far from the settled areas. Without great mobility, they were confined to the fringe of the desert and the steppe. Many centuries later the domestication of pack animals wrought a profound change. It was the use of the donkey, the dromedary, the Bactrian camel, and the horse that made true nomadism possible. The herdsman could now move his flocks away from the settled regions and into the heart of the desert and the steppe. These areas in the Middle East and Central Asia became home to a new type of farmer who planted no crops but kept his "fields on the hoof."

In other areas of the world, nomadism developed from different animal complexes—the reindeer or caribou in the north, the yak in Tibet, and the bison and the horse on the American plains. These animals seem very different from one another, but all have one thing in common—they thrive in dry areas.

It is well known that nomadism takes place in arid lands, but the precise nature of the relationship between the nomad and the land on which he depends has been frequently misunderstood. There is a common misconception that the nomad has been responsible for the very desert in which he lived—overgrazing. But contemporary studies of nomad land use have demonstrated just the opposite—they actually increase the fertility of these marginal areas through manuring. The Soviets eliminated the nomad from Kazakhstan with the result that this once great grassland has turned into a desert wasteland.

Only in Mongolia, where the greater part of the population is nomadic, has there been any interest in improving pastoral productivity. Most governments have been intent on eliminating or settling the nomad. They assume that the nomad is inefficient in utilizing the resources of the land. However, most of these lands cannot be farmed easily and pastoralism is often the most efficient utilization of what is already there. Modern attempts to convert these areas to farmland by irrigation have often proved unsuccessful or have been disastrous. In Iraq, irrigation of the Dujailah desert brought salts to the surface of the land, killing all plant life, and rendering this desert useless even to the nomad. Behind these policies is a basic lack of respect for a way of life that evolved over thousands of years to fit man and his animals to a delicate environment.

Although today we live in a world dominated by the settled, this was not always so. In the past there were periods when the nomads ruled their own lands as well as those of the settled. Settled wealth has always attracted nomad raiders. Their way of life made them good warriors, so periodically they swooped down and plundered these spots. The Great Wall of China was built to prevent these raids and the Pharaohs built a similar wall at Sinai.

But the settled cultures are now taking their revenge. Everywhere nomadism is on the wane. Borders are closing in on nomad migrations; nomad tribal power is being broken by central governments, and their pasture lands are being taken from them (just as was done to the American nomads of the Great Plains a hundred years ago). Nation states cannot tolerate a freely moving people who cross political borders at will, who evade taxation, and insist on their right to bear arms. Nomad life is very quickly being exterminated. Like the Israelites in the Land of the Pharaohs, the nomad is again being sold into slavery.

THE TENT AND THE NOMAD

According to the commandment of the LORD *they abode in their tents, and according to the commandment of the* LORD *they journeyed.*

—NUMBERS 9:20

The versatility of Kobuk Eskimos in constructing a temporary shelter is to be seen at present in the manipulation of a single piece of canvas to provide day-to-day changes in protection with each change of wind, precipitation and temperature. We have seen such a canvas converted in the course of a single day from a simple lean-to to a wall tent, to a hemispherical hut. It is well to remember that just at the time of Europeans, Kobuk people had no conception of a dwelling as a thing of permanence. Their houses and camps must have seemed less objects of property and sentiment than their canoes and their clothing. A dwelling was a temporary exploitation of natural resources and an expression of personality in a time of particular need.

—J. L. GIDDINGS, Kobuk River People

The nomad lives not so much in his tent as in the desert, the steppe, or the tundra. The tent is important as shelter, but not in the same way as our homes and workplaces are important to us. The nomad spends a great deal of time living and working under the open sky, for herding is by nature an outside activity. Clothing is often more vital to survival than shelter. Among some desert dwellers the young boys are sent off with the herds with nothing but the clothes on their backs. They sleep and live all year in the open with no shelter at all. Even the women do most of their work outside the tent if the weather permits. Looms, churns, and querns are more often seen outside the tent than in it.

The tent does not erect a clear boundary between inside and outside such as we are used to in our own housing. In bad weather the wind blows through the gaps of the tent cloth, rain leaks through the roof, or snow falls through the open smoke hole. But the nomad feels at home with these conditions and prefers this contact with the outdoors. Black-tent nomads are so accustomed to the feel of a flexible cloth roof over their heads that a solid roof constitutes a threat: There are many stories of how these nomads cannot at first sleep in a solid house for fear that the roof will fall and crush them. For the nomad, psychological protection—the feeling of security—is not tied to any absolute protection from the physical elements.

The space within the ordinary nomad tent is not large and so must be carefully organized. This organization is always a reflection of social organization and determines where people are seated and where possessions are kept. There is always a division between the men's and women's sides of the tent. The line between the sides may be quite strict, as in Arab cultures where there is a dividing curtain and where no adult male but the husband ever enters the women's side, or the line may be loose and people of both sexes may move about freely as with the Inuit. This division of the tent also constitutes a separation of the type of work for which each sex is responsible, so the looms, churns, and utensils are kept and used on the women's side while the saddles, harnesses, and weapons are kept on the men's side. In many tribes the women have a larger space for their half since they do more work under the tent roof than the men do. One of the most important things the women do in the tent is to make more tents. It is important to remember that it is the women who are the architects in nomad societies. The men may make the wooden parts, but since wood figures so little in most tent designs, it is the women as weavers, and as leather and bark workers who make and design the tent.

There is a definite order in the seating of residents and guests of the tent, always in accordance with a person's position in the social hierarchy. In tents that have a central hearth the place of honor is the warmest spot—between the fire and the back wall—while those of lesser prestige sit close to the drafty doorway. Among the Bedouin, the honored guest is seated close to the host. The dwelling places for the nomad's gods—the sacred areas—are always set in the warmest or most protected spot, close to the hearth or against the back wall.

The nomad's possessions are necessarily few since everything must be moved frequently, so each object has its exact place where it can be found the moment it is needed. Our own haphazard method of moving—with waylaid articles and mass confusion—would surely amuse the nomad. The nomad always knows where everything is, whether when on the move or when camped. All loose articles are stowed in boxes and bags. These containers are much like the tent itself—tough yet flexible. The woven bags or bent-wood boxes are as important as the tent itself: the tent shelters the nomad, the containers shelter his possessions. These bags and chests, along with mats, rugs, and cushions are all the furniture that the nomad needs—although a few nomad tribes use portable beds, and the tipi dwellers have their lazy-backs to lounge against.

Because the nomads must limit the quantity of possessions, each object is designed to fulfill as many functions as possible. This is especially true of the tent. The Netsilik Inuit turn their summer tent into a winter sled by rolling it up and pouring water on it which freezes solid. The Siberian Koryaks use their sleds to hold down the tent cover in the fierce winter winds. The Qashqai and the Plains Indians turn their tent poles into rafts to ferry themselves across the rivers they encounter on migration.

We have much to learn from the nomads about *living*. Our society is highly mobile, but we have adopted few of the tools that make nomadic life a pleasure. Even if we never live in a tent, there is much to be said for the nomad's way of life under the tent roof. What follows is an attempt to understand the tents of the nomad and the part it plays in their lives.

CHAPTER ONE

THE BLACK TENT

O children of Jerusalem, I am black, but of good grace, as the tents of Kedar and as the flaps of the tents of the Salmeens.

—SOLOMON 1 : 5

The black tent is the tent of the Bible, the Jews, and the Arabs, and a hundred other tribes scattered over Africa and Asia. Its mark upon these people cannot be reckoned. In the desert and the mountain, it had been their home, their temple, and sanctuary. Without this tent the people of the Middle East might never have ventured into the desert.

The birthplace of the black tent is probably somewhere near Mesopotamia. Its origin is tied to the domestication of goats and sheep, the animals that provided the material for the tent cloth and permitted the early nomads to begin their break from settled agriculture. These people were probably only seminomadic and tilled the soil part of the time. They moved their belongings on donkeys, and thus the distance they could travel was limited.

But with the domestication of the camel, a final break was made. The nomad could roam the desert, find pasture for his flocks, and never again till the soil. The camel could carry greater loads than the donkey, so the tent increased in size. The black tent and the camel moved together into the new lands so that their respective territories roughly coincide today. (The exception to this is the mat tent which will be considered later.)

The black tent moved out of its homeland until it had reached the Atlantic coast on one side and the eastern border of Tibet on the other. As it spread it was adapted to fit each particular environment it entered. In the mountains, where there was some rainfall, the roof was steeply pitched to shed rain; in the desert it was flattened and lowered to shield its inhabitants from sun and sand-

BLACK-TENT TERRITORY

after map from Feilberg.

storms. In hot country, it was made open to allow the air to blow through; in cold lands, it was completely enclosed. There is no single tent design that has adapted to such a range of environments. The black tent is found only in dry country, but within this arid zone it is found in almost every temperature range and in every type of terrain.

To do real justice to the black tent in all its diversity would require an encyclopedia—what I include here is but a brief outline of the subject. First, I will give a short introduction to black-tent construction; this will be followed by descriptions of specific tents and the peoples that use them.

SPINNING, WEAVING, SEWING

You shall also make the curtains of goats' hair for a tent over the tabernacle; eleven curtains shall you make. The length of each shall be thirty cubits, and the breadth of each curtain four cubits; the eleven curtains shall have the same measure.

—EXODUS 26:7

Black-tent dwellers are weavers. They weave not only the roofs, walls, and floors of their homes, but many of the furnishings as well. The wall cloths, spindle bags, carpet bags, and the carpets are all woven in rich colors and intricate geometrical designs. The carpets alone have made the tribal names of Kurd, Bakhtiari, Baluchi, Qashqai, and many others famous the world over as the technique of knotting used on these carpets was invented by these nomads.

YARN

The preferred fiber for almost all black tents is goat hair—only this fiber has the requisite strength and length. It is the particular tensile qualities of goat hair that gives the black tent its distinctive form. Many tents are made of pure goat hair, but often sheep or camel wool or a plant fiber are added. Pure sheep wool stretches too much under tension while camel hair is short and weak, thus a certain percentage of goat hair is always needed. The black tent obtains its "blackness" from the natural jet-black color of the goat's hair—however, many "black tents" are not black at all but are dyed other colors.

The wool or hair is spun into yarn on a simple drop spindle, which consists of a thin stick and a flywheel, the whorl. It is the earliest method of spinning known, and it has an advantage over the more complicated spinning wheel in that the spinner is free to move about and spin at the same time. Women spin while walking and on camelback, young girls spin while they play. The spinner keeps the wool under her arm, in the folds of her clothing, or up a sleeve. She pulls out a bunch, ties an end to the spindle, loops it under the hook at the end, and gives it a spin. The yarn twists to where it is held, the spindle falls to the ground; the spun yarn is then wound around the spindle and looped under the hook to begin again.

MAKING THE BLACK TENT

SHEARING

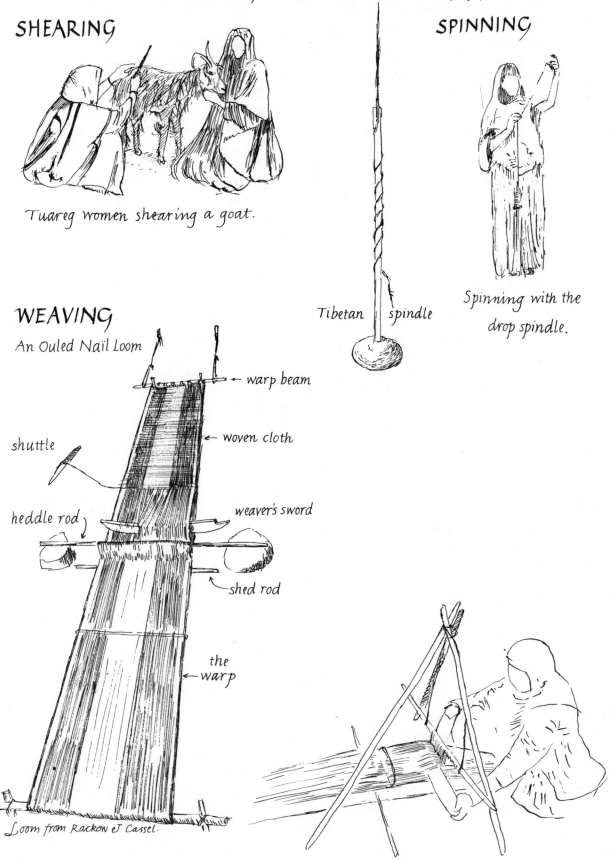

Tuareg women shearing a goat.

SPINNING

Tibetan spindle

Spinning with the drop spindle.

WEAVING

An Ouled Nail Loom

← warp beam

← woven cloth

shuttle

weaver's sword

heddle rod

← shed rod

the
← warp

Loom from Rackow eJ Cassel.

LOOM

The horizontal ground loom that weaves the fabric is basically the same throughout all of the black-tent territory. It is easy to construct, has few moving parts, and can be rolled up with any unfinished weaving when it's time to move. The warp is wound around two poles—the warp beams—set at the length of the desired cloth and held by four stakes. The heddles are made of string loops tied around alternate warp threads and the heddle stick which rests on a couple of rocks. A shed rod separates the warp. The weft is beaten down with a wide weaver's sword. As the weaving progresses the weaver conveniently sits on the woven part.

This loom is used to weave a variety of different types of cloth. Cloth for the roof and the tension bands is made with a tight weave to shed water, while that for the walls is made of a looser weave. In some areas, such as Morocco, the wall cloths are woven on a horizontal loom on which rugs are also woven.

The breadth of the woven cloth is the "modular unit" of black-tent construction. This system of construction is ancient: The "eleven curtains" of the tabernacle tent mentioned in Exodus are these very same cloth breadths. Note that the length and width—thirty cubits by four cubits—is carefully specified, indicating that this system was long in use at the time of Exodus. (A cubit equals the length of the forearm, approximately eighteen inches.)

While the cloth breadths are woven by women working alone, they are usually sewn together in a group. Since a new tent signifies a new tent family, it is always cause for celebration and feasting. The cloth breadths are sewn side by side to form a rectangle. Though the rectangle is made in many sizes and with many variations—it may be slightly wider in front or in back, and it may have extensions at some places—the basis for the tent is always the rectangle.

TENT CLOTH

The primary purposes of the black tent are: 1) to provide shade from the sun, 2) to protect from cold, wind, sand, and dust, and 3) to provide privacy for the occupants. The black color of the tent is functional: a black cover gives more shade. And while black absorbs more heat, the loose weave lets the heat disperse so that the interior may be twenty to thirty degrees cooler than the outside. Travelers in desert country have found that their canvas tents were considerably hotter than the black tent.

The tent cloth is like a thick heavy blanket. Although the weave is loose enough to see daylight through the cloth, it is fair as rain protection. When wet, the yarn swells—closing the holes—and the natural oiliness of the hair sheds the rain for a while. The tent will leak in a prolonged rain, but in the dry areas where the tent is used this is not a serious problem. The biggest problem of a wet tent for the nomads is that the weight of the tent becomes so great that the pack animals can barely move it.

Since the tent material is wool and hair, it does insulate from the cold. The Tibetan black tent made of yak hair is used in extremely cold country. Although the Tibetans prefer this tent, they will readily admit that the yurt is a warmer dwelling. What is amazing is that a tent that originated in a hot desert country could penetrate into such a cold land.

One-pole Sinai tent.

The weave of the black-tent walls do not offer the best wind protection. It is desirable to have the breezes blow through the tent when it is hot, but when it is cold, many black-tent dwellers set up reed, stone, or brush walls for additional protection from the winds. In addition, sheltered places are always chosen in the winter.

The life of tent cloth is from five to six years. In order to keep the material from rotting quickly, tents are pitched so that the lower edges don't touch the ground. Several tent-dwelling tribes add new cloth breadths to the middle of the tent each year, and thus the tent grows outward—by the time the cloth is worn out, it has reached the lower edge. The tent itself usually lasts as long as the tent family: A new tent is made at the start of a new family, and as long as the family survives the tent is renewed.

The tent cloth is stretched by means of rope stays made of wool, hair, or hemp (the latter is the strongest). The desert tribes use very long stays to take the shock of high winds. In the Eastern black-tent zone the stays attach directly to loops sewn to the edge of the tent cloth. The tents of the Western zone are more complicated: The stay is attached to a stay fastener which is itself fastened to a tension band. This method spreads the stress created by the stay over a wider area of the tent cloth. (More on these differences later.)

TENT FRAME

The black tent uses very little wood in its frame: Only a few other tents in the world, such as the Inuit ridge tents, use less. The minimal use of wood is possible because the black tent is a tensile structure ("tent" and "tensile" derive from the Latin *tendre,* to stretch). In tensile structures, all of the tension of the cover is collected in a few compression members—the poles. In the black tent, the great weight of the tent cloth and the great tension created by stretching the cloth is concentrated in the few vertical poles. This also means that the cover and the frame are interdependent—neither can stand without the other—and this interdependence makes it possible to use only a few poles. This system is in marked contrast to tents such as the yurt or tipi that have free-standing frames.

PERSIAN AND ARAB BLACK TENTS: THE BASIC TYPES

There are two basic types of black tent—the Eastern or Persian type and the Western or Arab type.* This division is a reflection of both a difference in tent

* This division follows the work of C. G. Feilberg, *La Tente Noire.*

construction and a difference in the geographical-cultural areas where the two types are found. The Persian type is found in the eastern half of black-tent territory running from Iran (Persia) to Tibet. These tents are of the simplest construction following the description I have just given—a series of cloth breadths, sewn side by side with loops at the edges for the rope stays. When the tent is set up the main pull of the ropes must be lengthwise (in the same direction of the seams) for if the pull was across the seams, it would pull them apart. The poles are generally placed under the seams, which can take the stress at this point. The Persian tent is used by the Irano-Afghan group of related peoples as well as the Tibetans at the easternmost extension of black-tent territory.

The Arab type of black tent is used by the Bedouin tribes of Arabia, Iraq, and Syria and all the tribes to the west of them, who adopted the black tent directly from them. This tent uses the same basic tent cloth as the Persian type but has the addition of tension bands sewn across the cloth breadths. Ropes attach to the tension bands so that the main pull of the ropes is across the seams— exactly the opposite to that of the Persian tent. The tension created by the pull of the ropes is concentrated in the tension bands. These bands, the poles that stand under them, and the rope stays all create an independent support system underneath the tent cloth.

The tension band must be a later development in the history of the black tent. Our earliest description of the black tent—the tabernacle cover described in Exodus—is of the Persian type: goat's hair cloth breadths sewn side by side, made in two parts, and joined down the middle with toggles and loops. In fact, this description fits exactly tents found in the Zagros Mountains of Iran today (see the Lur tent). However, the Semitic people who developed this tent weren't content with this simple rectangle of cloth. Probably because of the high winds they encountered in the desert, they developed the tension band as additional reinforcement of the tent cloth and turned the whole tent into a more sophisticated structure.

The cloth breadths are sewn edge to edge.

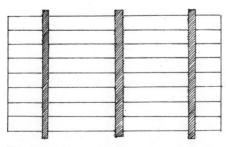

Tension bands are sewn across the cloth breadths.

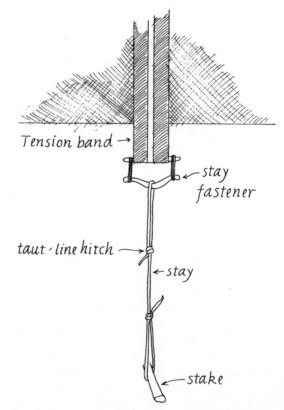

Tension band →

← stay fastener

taut-line hitch →

← stay

—stake

The people who today dwell in the homeland of the black tent are Bedouins. Their tent is a highly evolved design made exclusively for desert use. They themselves have a culture that is finely adapted to fit the desert environment—they are the "nomads of nomads" who travel faster and farther than any other black-tent nomads. For these reasons I will use the Bedouin and their tent as a starting place from which to examine the many different forms of the black tent and the cultures that use them. From Bedouin country we will move to North Africa and examine how the Bedouin tent changed in the hands of the North Africans. Last, we will look at the Persian-style black tent which is closest to the black tents of biblical times.

THE BEDOUIN

The Bedu place great value on austerity and asceticism. The harder one's life the less one eats and drinks—and this is minimal. The harder one drives oneself the greater one's esteem. So things of luxury are usually scorned. One would rather sit on the ground than a seat; one would rather sit upright than sprawl; one must give, not take. Generosity is paramount; one must share what food one has with anyone who was near, which meant that I was short of food, for the curious constantly surrounded me.

—PAUL VERITY, *The Kababish*

Ahl el beit they call themselves—"people of the tent." The Bedouin pride themselves as being the only true *arabs* or "tent dwellers," which the word *arab* means. Wandering Bedouin can be found over almost all of black-tent territory,

but the traditional tribal areas are Arabia, the Sinai, and parts of present day Jordan, Syria, Israel, and Iraq. Bedouin tribesmen spread Islam and the Arabic language from the Pyrenees to the Himalayas. The Bedouin are Ishmaelites who, like the Jews, trace their descent back to the biblical patriarch Abraham—himself a nomad.

The "true" Bedouin are exclusively camel breeders. This places them in a special position among the other desert dwelling peoples. It gives them the mobility to range the desert and to control the movement of all others within their territory. In the past, the oasis dwellers as well as the caravan trade had to buy protection in Bedouin territory. The noble Bedouin was first of all a warrior who spent much time in raiding camel herds of others and in protecting his own. Raiding was always done according to a code that specified certain people as noncombatants—women, children, and blacksmiths. Thus, the truly productive members of society were not disrupted by warfare.

The tribes of Central Arabia, such as the Rualla and the Al Murrah, are just such full-time camel breeders who have mastered the art of living in the desert interior where others could never survive. Their existence depends on a knowledge of the wells hidden in their territory, fast communication about the locations of new pasture, and the ability to travel fast. The Al Murrah can move at the rate of forty miles a day and have been known to journey 1,200 miles—the length of Saudi Arabia—in search of winter pasture.

The Bedouin classify the tribes of their country according to how nomadic they are. The *swaja* are the shepherd tribes who tend the flocks of goats and sheep. They are considered *arabs* but not *bedouin*. They are full-time tent dwellers and they often own camels, but they can never move as far or as fast as the Bedouin since the flocks must be kept within a day or two of water. Below the swaja are the *ra'w*—the seminomads who have flocks but also till the land. They live under the tent for only part of the year and spend the rest of their time in settled villages. The sedentary village dwellers—the *karawne*—are at the bottom of the hierarchy. They are the oasis farmers who grow dates, grain, and vegetables. They are often tenant farmers on Bedouin-owned land.

In all of these tribes it is actually women, children, servants, and slaves who do most of the real work. It is they who pitch the tents, cook, carry water, spin and weave, and look after the flocks. Protecting the herds and raiding used to take up much of the nobleman's time, but now that raiding is ended, the men sit and drink coffee, search out new pastures, and hunt. Some now work in the oil fields and mines, and the old way of life is fast eroding. Trucks and cars are replacing the camel, and newly dug wells are upsetting traditional water rights. Some Arabian Bedouin now hire big trucks to carry the women and children, and tent, and all the furnishings to new pasture lands which the men follow with the herds.

Bedouin life is regulated by the seasons. Summer is a time of drought and the Bedouin are obliged to camp near wells or permanent streams since even the camels must be watered once every four days. These camps are set up near the oases where the nomads exchange wool and milk products for dates, grain, cloth, and weapons before returning to the desert. The summer camp is tightly packed so that all will be near water, and the tents are pitched so that the rope stays are almost touching.

In the fall the rains come and the Bedouin return to their desert home for nine months. Camps are now small—four to five tents—and spread out because the pasture is widely dispersed. If the pasture is lush, the flocks only have to be watered once every four days so they can be moved far from the wells. As pasture thins out, thunderstorms are watched for and scouts are sent to find the spot where the rain fell—locations that will shortly become green pasture.

Sandy spots are always preferred for camping. The sand absorbs the refuse of the camp and when the camp is moved the shifting sand covers all. Camps are changed at least every ten days if possible as the filth accumulates and makes the campsite unbearable.

Anyone entering a Bedouin camp is made welcome and must be given food and shelter for at least three days as desert law decrees. Bedouin hospitality is proverbial: The host will readily slaughter his last sheep to honor a guest. Bedouin on the verge of starvation have been known to give away their last food, saying that they have plenty.

THE CAMEL

Allah created the desert so that he could wander in peace, but he saw his error and corrected it. And so to the shame of his enemies and for the use of mankind the camel was created.

—BEDOUIN SAYING

The camel is a true desert animal. It thrives on thorny plants that other animals reject, its feet act like snow shoes in the sand, and it will plod through the desert at the steady rate of three miles an hour with five to eight hundred pounds on its back. The dromedary, or one-humped camel, was first domesticated in Arabia, the homeland of the Bedouin. To the Bedouin the camel is life itself—it provides milk and meat, and in an emergency the stomach fluid can save a traveler from thirst. Bedouins can go for months without water, drinking only camel's milk, as the camels drink water unfit for humans. Camel wool is used for clothing, the dung for fuel, and the skins for water bags and sandals. The men wash their hands in camel urine on cold mornings; the women wash their hair in it to kill lice, and Bedouin newborn are baptized with it. The Bedouin count their wealth in camels and can identify any camel in their herd by its tracks. The list of camels named according to age, color, breed, and gait is endless, and the Bedouin never tire of talking about them.

It is no accident that the territory of the black tent and the dromedary roughly coincide, for it was the camel that provided the back that made it possible to carry so heavy a tent. And it was the camel that enabled the nomad to scout out far-flung pastures, which made it possible to keep large flocks of sheep and goats, which, in turn, provided wool and hair for the tent and its furnishings. These three—the camel, the sheep, and the goat—provided the material basis for Middle Eastern nomadism.

THE BEDOUIN TENT

The Aarab tent, which they call the beyt *(pl.* byut) *es-shaar, "abode, booth, or house of hair," that is of black worsted or hair cloth, has with its pent roof, somewhat the form of a cottage. The tent-stuff, strong and rude, is defended by a list sewed under at the heads of the am'dan, and may last out, they say, a generation, only wearing thinner: but when their roof-cloth is threadbare it is a feeble shelter, thrilled by the darting beams of the Arabian sun, and casting only a grey shadow. The Arabian tent strains strongly upon all the staves, and in good holding-ground, may resist the boisterous blasts which happen at the crises of the year, especially in some deep mountainous valleys. Even in the weak sand the tents are seldom overblown.*

—CHARLES M. DOUGHTY, *Travels in Arabia Deserta*

The Bedouin tent is the most widespread of black-tent designs and the most refined for desert use. The Danish scholar C. G. Feilberg, who wrote the definitive book on the black tent, considers this tent design the culmination of black-tent evolution. It is a tent finely adapted to its desert environment: the roof is flattened and given an aerodynamic shape so that the wind cannot take hold, and there is minimal use of wood—the ridgepole, which is quite large in other black tents, has been reduced to a small circular plaque. The tension bands are the minimum required, and the rope stays are long.

The Bedouin calls the tent *beit sha'r*—house of hair. The tent cloth is woven of pure goat hair or of a mixture of goat and sheep or camel wool. The woven cloth breadths are sewn together, the number and length depending on

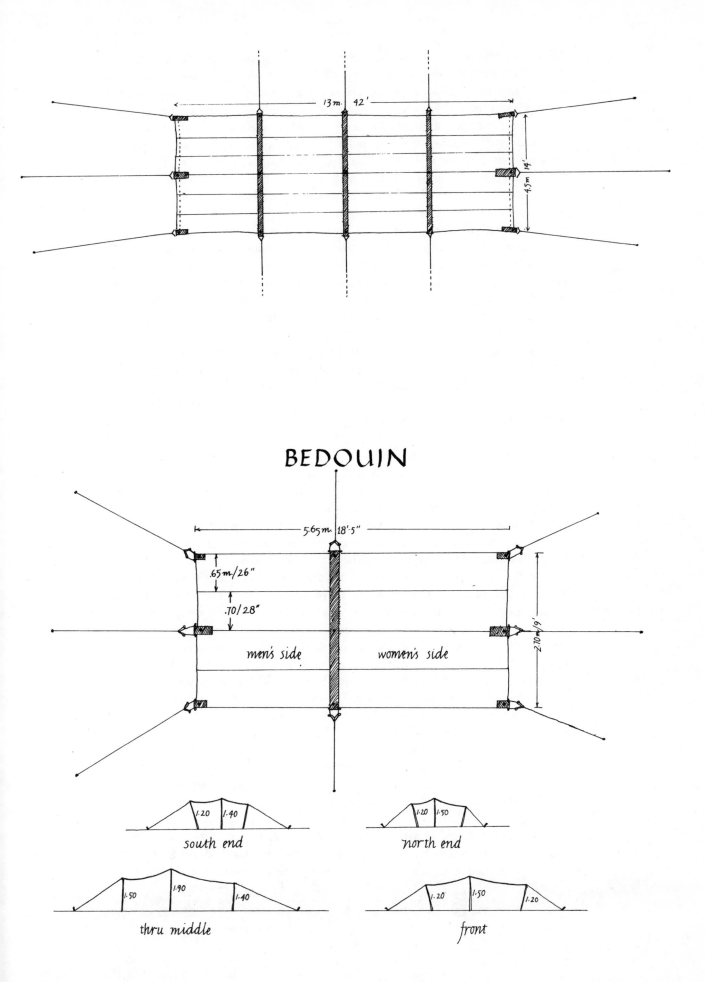

BEDOUIN

men's side   women's side

13 m. 42'
14'
4.5 m

5.65 m. 18'·5"
.65 m/26"
.70/28"
2.70 m/9'

south end

1·20 1·40

north end

1·20 1·50

thru middle

1·50 1·90 1·40

front

1·20 1·50 1·20

the wealth and status of the tent owner. A poor Arab may have only two breadths, twenty feet long for his tent, while a rich sheik may use six breadths seventy feet long. Tension bands are sewn across the breadths, the number depending on the relative size of the tent. Each band is supported by three poles —a seven-foot-high center pole flanked by another on each side. The tent size is reckoned by the number of center poles (exclusive of the end ones) so that the poor tent has but one, while the sheik's tent has four. If the tent cloth is larger than eight breadths, it is made in two parts to keep each section within a camel's load. These large tents are only seen in semipermanent camps as the tent cloth is too difficult to move frequently.

At the end of each tension band there is a stay fastener and rope stay. The stay fasteners are made of wood or leather in a great variety of shapes: bent and forked stick-stay fasteners are used by the shepherd tribes (*swaja*), while braided leather loops are used by camel-breeding tribes such as the Rualla. The rope stays of hemp are made very long—one hundred feet or more. This length helps absorb the shock of sudden winds and transfers the pull on the stakes so that it is perpendicular to them. The long stays also provide protection against raiders riding through camp—they trip the horses or camels. If two tents are pitched so that the ropes cross, the households are united in some way. Fines are often levied according to the number of ropes on the offender's tent.

Bedouin east of the Dead Sea sacrifice a sheep in the spot where they pitch the tent. The tent is always pitched by women: the ground is cleared of stones and shrubs and made as level as possible, then the tent is unrolled and spread over this place, and the ropes are pulled out and staked. From long experience the women can judge exactly where to place the stakes. A corner pole is then pushed up in place; next, the poles along one side, followed by the center poles. When all the poles are in place and the roof is aloft, the wall curtains are pinned in place and the carpets and other tent furnishings are brought in. Within an hour the tent is ready and the hearth fires are blazing.

Arabs pitch their tents facing either east toward Mecca or south so that the back wall is set against the northern winds and the men's side is toward the east. The direction of the tent depends on the particular tribal practice and the prevailing conditions at the time. In hot weather the tent is left completely open, the roof serving as a sunshade, but usually wall curtains (*ruag*) are pinned up for privacy and to keep out the wind and sand. These curtains can be moved to either side of the tent depending on wind direction and a variety of enclosures can be created by hanging them out on the ropes. The ruag, made of a looser weave than the roof cloth, are woven with red and black geometric designs. There is a piece of sack cloth at the bottom which can be buried in the sand or held down with rocks to seal out drafts. In Syria reed mats are often used for the outside walls. The dividing curtain (*qata*) separating the men's and women's sides, has the most elaborate designs woven into it—especially the end that extends out in front and is draped over the front ropes for all to see. In bad weather this end is brought across the front of the women's side, completely enclosing it.

A stranger should always approach the tent from the front. On approaching the tent one hears the pounding of the brass mortar and pestle as coffee beans are ground and mixed with cardamon. As the guests are seated in the

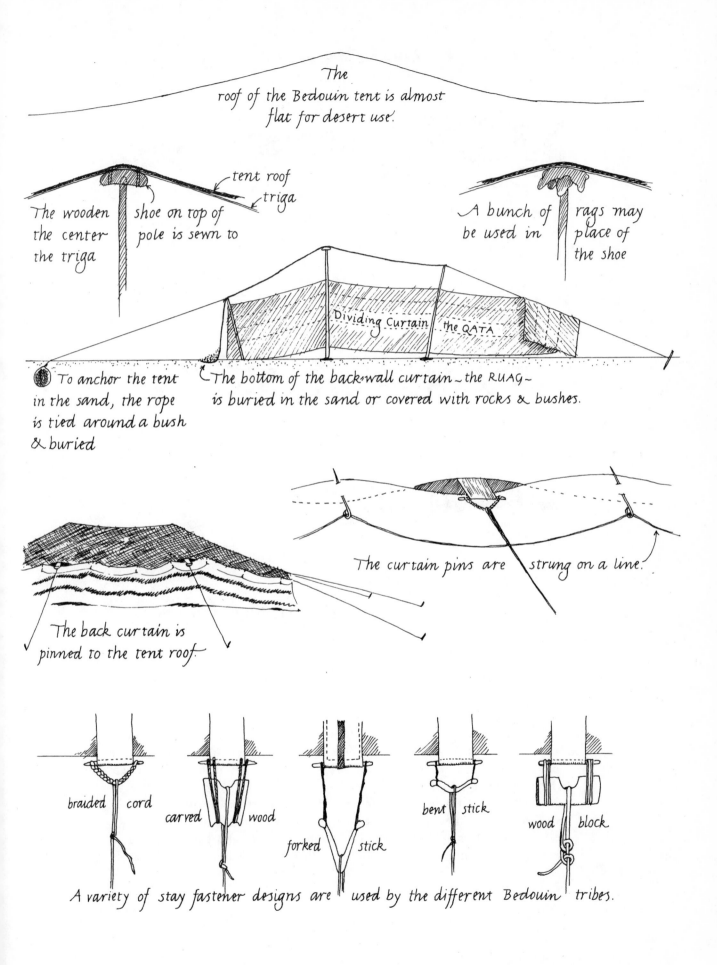

The
roof of the Bedouin tent is almost
flat for desert use.

tent roof
triga

The wooden shoe on top of
the center pole is sewn to
the triga the triga

A bunch of rags may
be used in place of
the shoe

Dividing Curtain the QATA

To anchor the tent
in the sand, the rope
is tied around a bush
& buried

The bottom of the back-wall curtain – the RUAG –
is buried in the sand or covered with rocks & bushes.

The curtain pins are strung on a line.

The back curtain is
pinned to the tent roof.

braided cord

carved wood

forked stick

bent stick

wood block

A variety of stay fastener designs are used by the different Bedouin tribes.

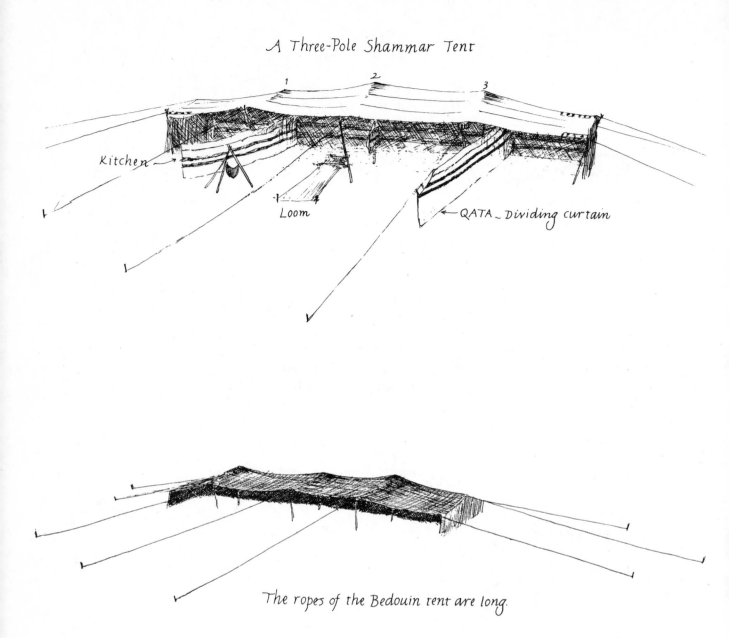

A Three-Pole Shammar Tent

Kitchen

Loom

QATA — Dividing curtain

The ropes of the Bedouin tent are long.

men's side, the coffee is brewed in a small hearth set just outside the tent. Coffee making and drinking are conducted as a ritual of desert hospitality: to be polite, the guest must drink at least three cups. If a cup of coffee is refused, the host empties it on the ground, for pride demands that man cannot accept what another has rejected.

The floor of the men's side is covered with carpets and mattresses for the guests to sit on. The host's camel saddle, covered with a sheepskin, is set on the rear mattress. This is a key piece of furniture—the host and guest of honor sit on either side of it and talk across it; the other guests sit in a semicircle facing them.

SETTING UP CAMP

Enlarge the place of thy
tent, & let them stretch
forth the curtains of
thine habitations : spare
not, lengthen the cords
& strengthen the stakes.

Isaiah 54:2

"Spread out the tent, oh my people;
stretch out the ropes;
drive in the pegs;
tighten the ropes, oh my children."

"Raise the majadin." (the front side pole)

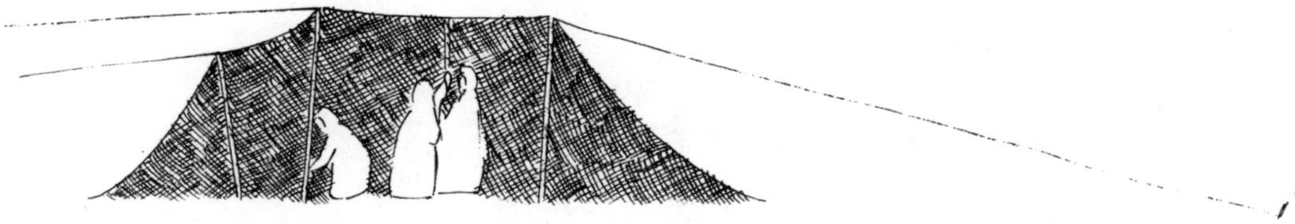

"Raise the center poles."

The women's side of the tent is bigger. It is the living and working area of the tent and is never seen by men other than the tent owner in accord with the traditional separation of sexes and seclusion of women. The women talk, cook, and weave on their side. In one corner of the women's side sits the camel litter in which they ride when the tribe migrates. The litter consists of a framework fastened to a camel saddle enclosed with cloth—a tent on camel back. Against the dividing curtain (qata) are stacked rugs and rolls of bedding, while near the far wall a bed of stones supports bags of grain and wool. The sleeping area is encircled with a border of stones. Saddlebags hang from tent poles and a hammock cradle may be stretched between them. The loom for weaving the tent cloth is set up with the warp running out the front of the tent. Outside the tent near the front corner goatskin water bags rest on a bed of bushes and a tripod suspends a goatskin churn. Nearby, the cooking hearth is made of three stones with iron bars set across to support cooking pots and bread pans.

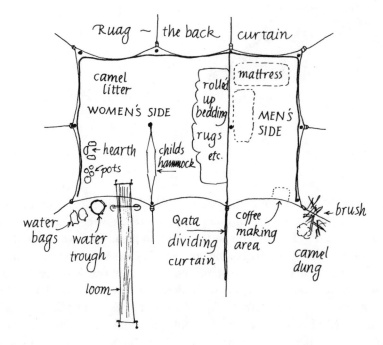

Ruag ~ the back curtain

camel litter

WOMEN'S SIDE

rolled up bedding rugs etc.

mattress

MEN'S SIDE

hearth

pots

childs hammock

water bags

water trough

Qata dividing curtain

coffee making area

brush

camel dung

loom

BREAKING CAMP

The tent is taken down, folded & rolled into a bundle that goes onto the back of a pack camel. Another camel carries the poles in a special pack saddle.

The tent belongs to the husband but is always under the wife's control. If a man has more than one wife, he must provide a tent for each. The tent is regarded as a sanctuary and the host is obliged to protect any who set foot in his tent and ask assistance. Even if this person is his enemy, he must provide at least three days of hospitality and guarantee safe passage in his tribal territory. It is considered unlawful to shoot a man in his tent.

In front of each tent or camp a mark is scored in the ground that indicates the *masjid,* or communal prayer ground. The prayer leader stands in front of the loop facing Mecca. The Arab religion is not tied to a particular place in the tent or spot on the ground—except for Mecca. A space becomes sacred when a devotee places his or her prayer rug there and faces toward Mecca.

When the tents are folded and the camp has moved, all that is left are the hearth stones, but these stay in place for years and leave evidence of the size and type of camp. The size and depth of the coffee hearth tells the observer whether the host was a generous man and even what tribe camped here.

TRANSITIONAL FORMS

Two Bedouin tribes have a tent different from the one just described: the Ouled Ali, who dwell in Libya, and the Kababish, who live to the south of them in the Sudan. The Ouled Ali tent has more pitch to the roof giving it prominent peaks, unlike those of the Arabian tents, but most noteworthy are the two cloth loops sewn at either end of the tent. These "extra" tension bands are important because they will be found running the whole length of the tent in other North African black tents. This tent is transitional between the Arabian Bedouin and the other North African black tents.

The Kababish tent is related to the Ouled Ali tent in that it has two tension bands, but the feature that most distinguishes it from the Arabian tent is the frame system, which consists of four forked center poles—two in the middle,

OULED ALI

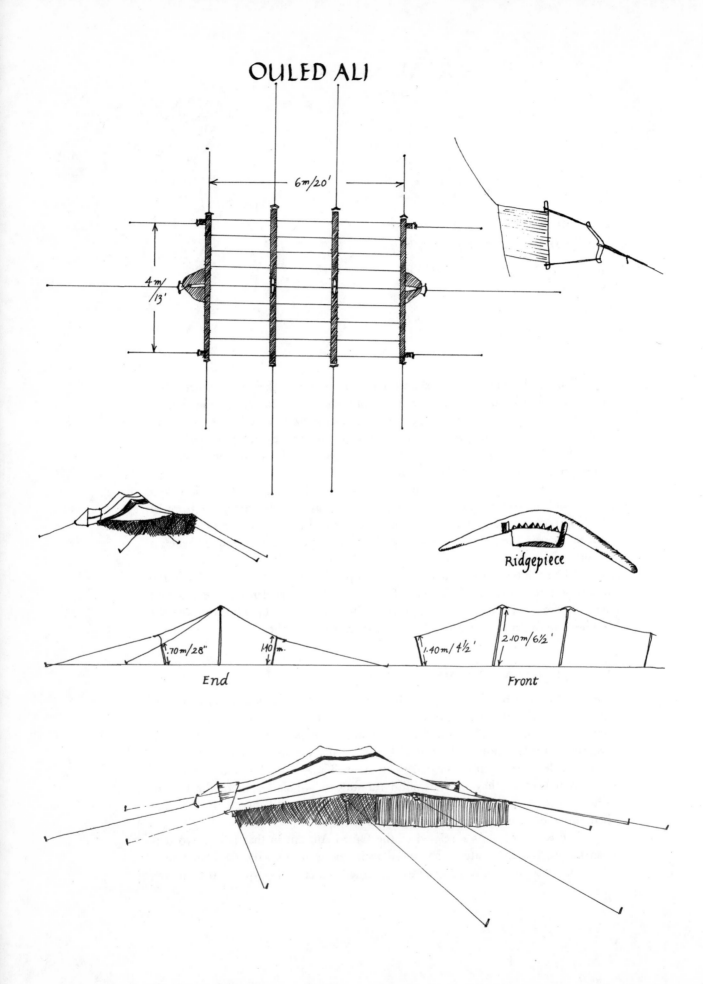

6m/20'

4m/13'

.70 m/28"

1.40 m.

1.40 m/4½'

2.10m/6½'

End

Front

Ridgepiece

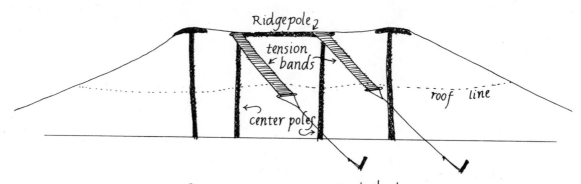

Support system for a Kababish tent.

which support a long ridgepole, and two on the ends, which support a short curved ridgepiece. This frame is similar to those used in the mat tents of people such as the Tuareg who live to the west and south of the Kababish. The Kababish live at the southern edge of black-tent territory bordering mat-tent territory (a few Kababish even use the mat tent). The Kababish tent is transitional between the black tent and the mat-and-skin tents which will be examined in the next chapter.

NORTH AFRICA

The Berbers were the original inhabitants of North Africa. They dwell there still, but beginning in the seventh century successive waves of Arab conquerors swept across North Africa changing the religion to Islam and the language to Arabic. All Berbers were influenced by Arabic culture but not in the same way. Some Berber tribes kept their culture relatively pure by moving south into the Sahara. (The Tuaregs and the Tibu are examples of this, because they did not adopt the black tent, retained instead their traditional mat-and-skin tents.) Other Berber tribes resisted Arab dominance by keeping to isolated mountain valleys. Some tribes, such as the Moors, were the result of a mixture of Berber and Arab. Still other Berbers were forced to become oasis farmers working for Arab nomad masters. The Berber culture was thus affected by varying degrees of Arab influence.

NORTH AFRICAN TRIBES

The nomads of North Africa dwell in two basically different environments, the mountain and desert, each demanding a different type of nomadism. The mountain nomads follow a short and regular migration cycle, up into the mountains in the summer and down to the valleys and plateaus in the winter. Summer is the principal time when the flocks are fattened on lush mountain pastures watered by melting snows. All of the animal products—lamb and kid wool, hair, milk, and meat—are produced at this time. By autumn the pastures are thin and the flocks have to be moved down to the plateaus for the winter. In wintertime the flocks get little to eat and the nomads move very little. It is the time to make and repair tents and to weave carpets; it is the time of large camps and great feasts and celebrations.

Most mountain nomads are seminomads who combine pastoralism with cultivation. Crops are planted in the spring, left for the summer, and harvested in the fall. Many of these people are transhumants who live in a stone house during the winter and a tent in the summer, although some do just the opposite. And some do not migrate at all, but leave the flocks in the care of hired shepherds.

While the mountain nomad travels on donkey back, his desert cousin favors the camel, as the desert nomad must travel farther and move more often. His seasonal pattern is just opposite to that of the mountain nomad. Winter is the time of fresh pasture when flocks are fattened; the nomads spread out with

Tent of the Zemmour

A Beni Mguild shepherd, his flocks & tent, Atlas Mtns.

single tent family camps often as much as ten miles from each other and thirty miles from the nearest water in order to find sufficient pasture. In summertime the nomad camps near the oasis to supervise the date harvest if he owns date groves. Some nomads even own houses there, but they pitch their tents in the courtyards and use the houses only for storage and receptions. The tent is always more comfortable than a house in the summer in the desert.

Caravan trade used to be an important source of wealth for the desert dweller—whether guiding the caravans or raiding them. The nomads used to control all commerce between the Mediterranean coast and the South Sahara. Now, with raiding ended by the central governments, some enterprising nomads have set up truck lines with stores along them so that they can stay nomadic while still conducting business.

The desert nomad lives a precarious existence. Periodically a drought forces some group to leave the desert and seek a new home. Invariably the mountain pastures attract them, and there is a conflict with a tribe already there. If the mountain nomads lose, they may take to the desert and the cycle begins all over again.

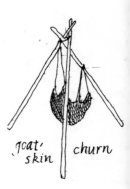

goat skin churn

NORTH AFRICAN TENTS

The North African Berbers adopted the black tent directly from the Bedouins who invaded their country. They took the distinguishing feature of the Bedouin tent—the tension band—and worked out a good many of the ways it could be used. Most of these tents have three tension bands and a large center one, the *triga,* which runs over the ridgepole and holds up the center poles. These three elements—the triga, the ridgepole, and the center poles—are the core features of the North African tents. They give the North African black tent its characteristic profile of a high curved ridge line. Each Berber or Arab tribe, cut off in its mountain or desert isolation, developed its own distinctive design—the variations go far beyond what I include here.

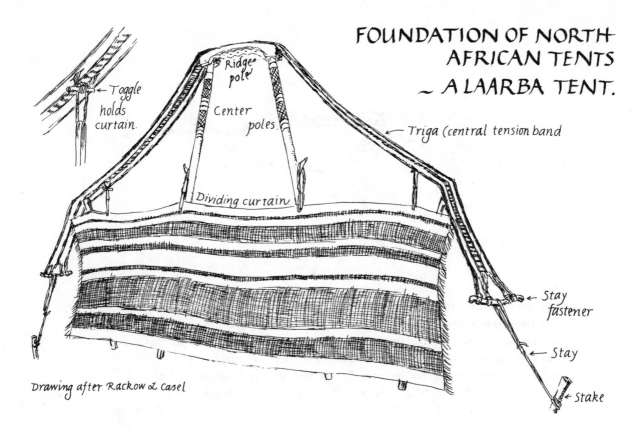

Ridge pole

←Toggle holds curtain.

Center poles

←Triga (central tension band

Dividing curtain

←Stay fastener

←Stay

←Stake

Drawing after Rackow & Casel

THE MOROCCAN BERBER TENT

The Moroccan Berber tent is used by tribes who inhabit the Atlas mountains. The mountains receive a heavier rainfall than most black tent areas, so the tent roof is given a fair amount of pitch. The tent is made in a variety of sizes, and unusually large tents are made for tribal chiefs for special occasions.

The tent cloth is made of goat hair with a small amount of sheep wool mixed in. (The poor mix in a liberal amount of palm fiber or make their tent out of palm fiber woven with cloth strips.) Unlike most black-tent peoples, the Berber men sew the woven breadths together. When the roof cloth is finished it is spread out on the ground and water is sprinkled over it in hope that this tent will attract rain—giving its occupants good pasture. The ends of the roof cloth are left with a fringe which helps the rain flow off the roof edge.

The wall curtains are four or five feet wide and woven on the upright loom on which rugs are woven. The weave of the wall cloth is fairly open since it doesn't have to shed water. The woven cloths are dyed in a bath of pomegranate skin and copper sulfate which turns them a deep black.

The cloth breadths last scarcely five years at which time they begin to leak badly. Each year in October the tent cloth is separated at the middle and two new breadths are added. Thus, the tent grows outward, and the tent as a whole lives as long as it is renewed.

The wall curtains are fastened to the edge of the roof with iron pins. In winter reed or rush mats are added outside these as protection from the wind and cold. An array of sacks, chests, cedar planks, corrugated iron, or stones are used to make low walls to keep out drafts and hold the wall cloths off the damp ground. If there is much rain the tent is trenched.

The key to the Moroccan tent is the ridgepole supported by two center poles. It not only supports the tent but is a symbol of protection—a benevolent force that guards the tent family. Its underside is carved with geometric designs and painted. The cedar center poles are also carved and between them hang religious charms to protect the tent. Stretched over them is a woven band, eight to sixteen inches wide, the triga, which holds up the ridgepole and imparts to the tent its characteristic shape—that of a vessel turned upside down.

Custom decrees that the tent must never be pitched in its old location. The women always put up the tent: A space is cleared of rocks and brush, the tent cloth is rolled out, and the stakes are pounded in with a wooden mallet—first the triga, then the four corners. A woman then slides under the tent cloth and pushes up the ridgepole with the center poles. If the stakes are set wrong she either digs beneath poles or puts rocks under them. The curtains are then pinned on and the family belongings are brought inside.

All of the North Africa Berbers pitch their tents in a sacred order—the *douar* or "circle." The typical douar is composed of fourteen to twenty-five

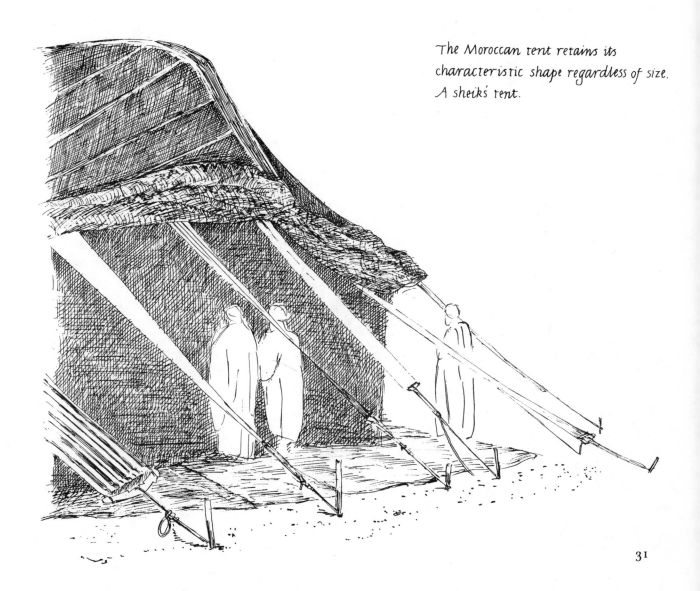

The Moroccan tent retains its characteristic shape regardless of size. A sheik's tent.

MOROCCAN BERBER

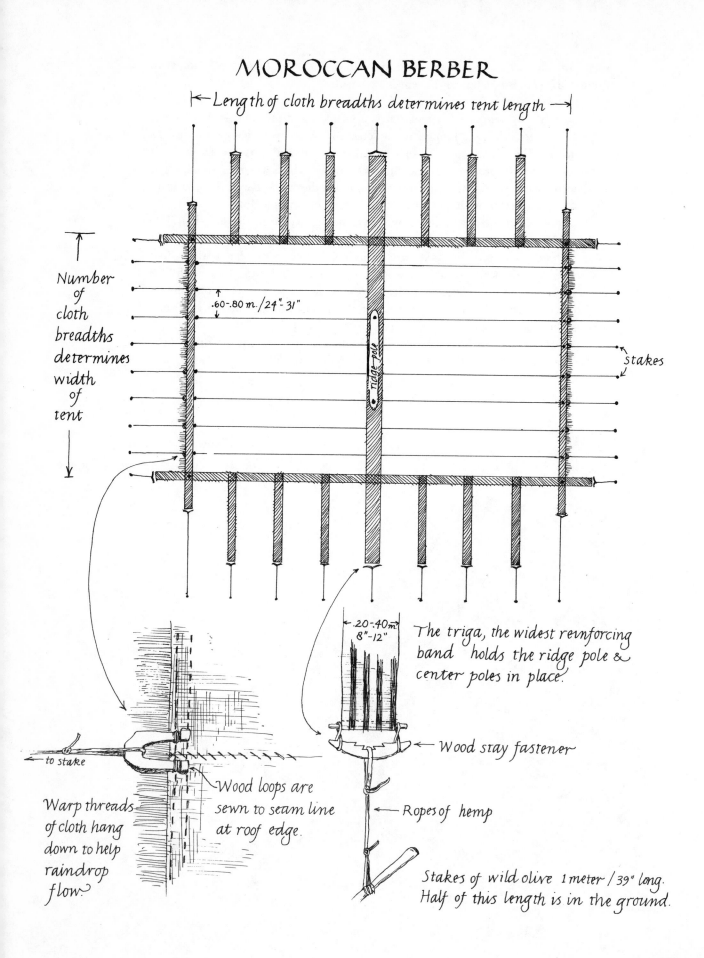

|← Length of cloth breadths determines tent length →|

Number of cloth breadths determines width of tent

.60-.80 m./24"-31"

ridge-pole

stakes

.20-.40 m. 8"-12"

The triga, the widest reinforcing band holds the ridge pole & center poles in place.

← Wood stay fastener

→ to stake

Wood loops are sewn to seam line at roof edge.

← Ropes of hemp

Warp threads of cloth hang down to help raindrop flow.

Stakes of wild olive 1 meter / 39" long. Half of this length is in the ground.

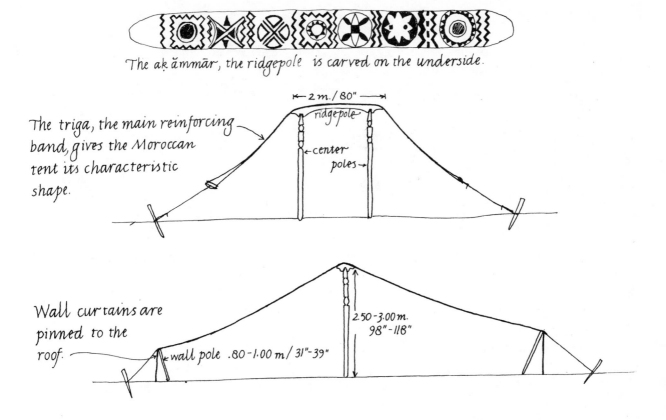

The aḳ ămmār, the ridgepole is carved on the underside.

← 2 m. / 80" →

ridgepole

←center poles→

The triga, the main reinforcing band, gives the Moroccan tent its characteristic shape.

2.50 - 3.00 m.
98" - 118"

Wall curtains are pinned to the roof.

wall pole .80 -1.00 m / 31"-39"

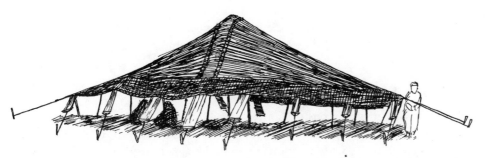

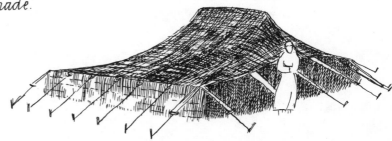

Front view of a tent in summer. The wall curtains are thrown up on the roof to let the breeze blow through. The tent becomes an open sun shade.

A Zemmour tent in winter. Reed mats are put over the walls to break the wind & insulate. Bushes or boards may be used in addition.

77310

FERNALD LIBRARY
COLBY-SAWYER COLLEGE
NEW LONDON, N.H. 03257

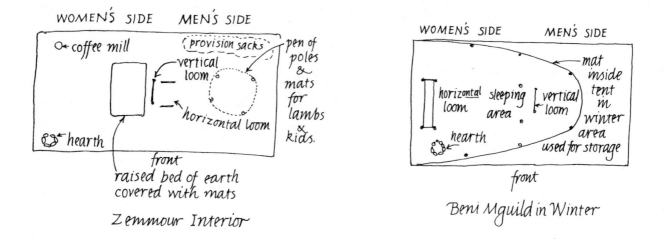

WOMEN'S SIDE   MEN'S SIDE

coffee mill   provision sacks   pen of poles & mats for lambs & kids.
        vertical loom
        horizontal loom
hearth

front
raised bed of earth
covered with mats

Zemmour Interior

WOMEN'S SIDE   MEN'S SIDE

horizontal loom   sleeping area   vertical loom   mat inside tent in winter area used for storage
        hearth

front

Beni Mguild in Winter

tents of related families. Brush is piled between the tents to keep the flocks in the douar at night. Each tent has its entrance facing the center of the douar where the mosque tent stands. This tent is referred to as the "center pole" of the douar —supporting it morally and spiritually—and is used as both a religious school and a sanctuary for travelers.

The douar is a survival of the early Berber village before the Arabs arrived. Although the North African names for the parts of the black tent are Arabic, those that apply to the douar are Berber. In the summer months the members of the douar divide into small groups and travel up to highland pastures.

ALGERIAN BLACK TENTS

Algerian tents are similar in basic construction to the Moroccan Berber tent. The narrow end and back reach almost to the ground so that no separate wall curtains are needed. These tents, with so many poles pushing out from the inside, have a squat, almost bloated appearance. Tents of the mountain tribes are larger than the desert tents, a reflection of the tribes' larger flocks. There are differences between each tribal design, but on the whole these tents are quite similar to each other and obviously related.

A douar in the Atlas.
The tents are placed in a circle. The spaces between are filled with brush to keep the flocks inside.

OULED NAÏL

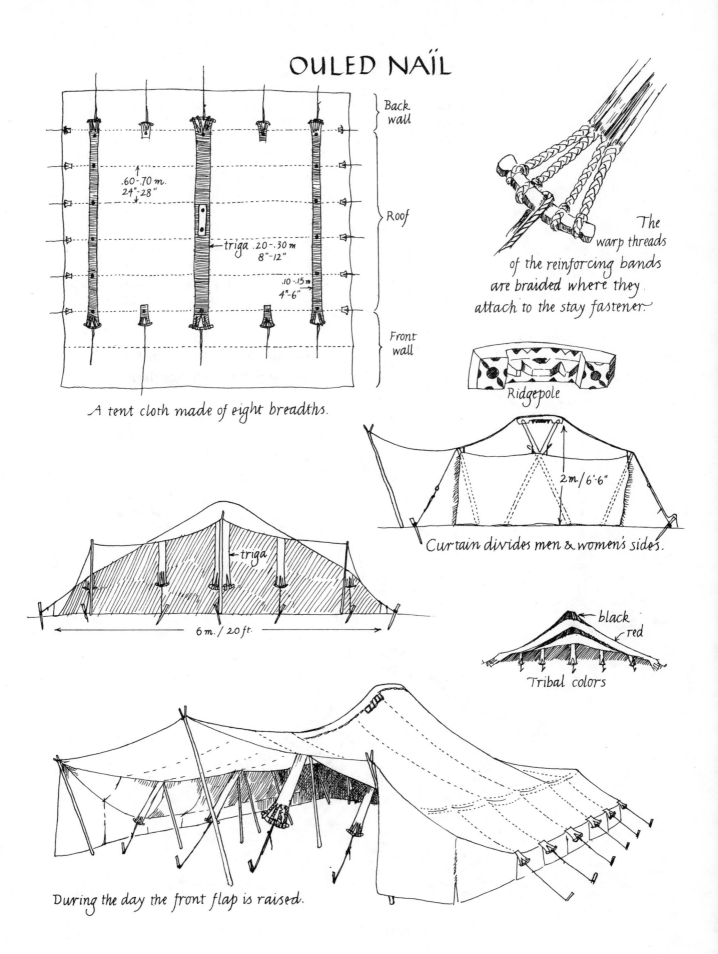

.60-.70 m.
24"-28"

triga .20-.30 m
8"-12"

.10-.15 m
4"-6"

Back wall

Roof

Front wall

A tent cloth made of eight breadths.

The warp threads of the reinforcing bands are braided where they attach to the stay fastener.

Ridgepole

2 m./6'-6"

Curtain divides men & women's sides.

triga

6 m. / 20 ft.

black
red

Tribal colors

During the day the front flap is raised.

DJEBEL AMOUR

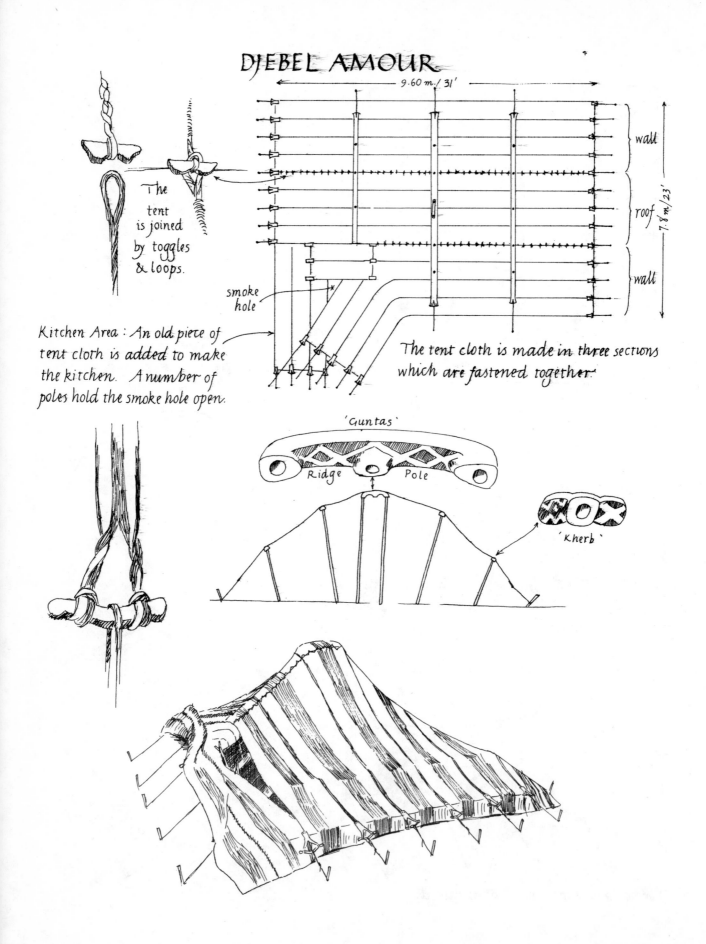

9.60 m. / 31'

7.8 m. / 23'

wall

roof

wall

The tent is joined by toggles & loops.

smoke hole

Kitchen Area : An old piece of tent cloth is added to make the kitchen. A number of poles hold the smoke hole open.

The tent cloth is made in three sections which are fastened together.

'Guntas'

Ridge   Pole

'Kherb'

CHAAMBA

DJEBEL NEFOUSA

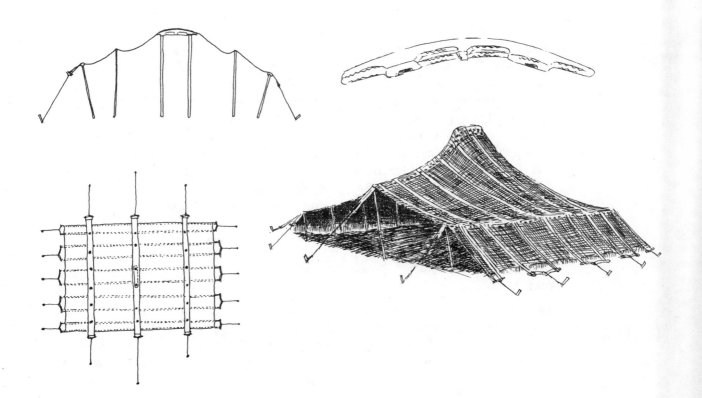

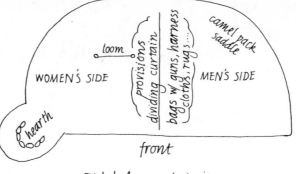

Djebel Amour Interior

The cloth breadths (*flij*) are woven of goat hair, with some sheep or palm fiber mixed into the weft, in widths ranging from two to three feet and lengths of thirty to sixty feet. The warp threads are usually dyed before weaving, and each tribe or clan has its own particular pattern of stripes so that each tribe can be identified by the color of its tent. The Ouled Naïl color the center warp a brown-black with a reddish-brown stripe on either side. Nemencha tents are striped red, brown, and black; the Chaamba black and gray.

Women sew the cloth breadths together with goat-hair thread and hem the ends. Large tents are made in three sections and fastened together with toggles and loops. Like the Moroccan tent, there are three tension bands with a ridge- and center poles. Unlike the Moroccan tent the side tension bands are sewn back from the edge so that a low wall hangs from the tension band when the tent is pitched.

Three rows of cedar poles support the tension bands with a short ridgepole at the center. The front and the back of the tent have loops sewn to them so that they can be raised or lowered with poles according to wind direction.

The tent is divided into men's and women's sides by means of a curtain suspended from the center poles and the triga. Another curtain extends across the front of the women's side to hide it from view. The Djebel Amour add an extension made of old cloth off a corner of the women's side for a kitchen with a hearth at its center. An opening is left where the cloths join which is held open by poles to make a smoke hole. (This is the only case of a smoke hole in any black tent except the Tibetan tent. Generally the cooking is done outside the tent.) The row of poles nearest the rear and side walls mark off a storage room for provisions. On the men's side guns, harnesses, clothes, and rugs are set against the dividing curtain and camel pack saddles are set against the back wall. A shallow hearth for making tea is dug just outside the front.

The principal differences in the Algerian tent derive from the way in which the tension bands are sewn across the cloth breadths. The Djebel Amour sew four breadths for a roof section and four for each wall. The Ouled Naïl sew five for the roof, two for the front flap, and one for the back wall.

THE MOOR TENT

The tents of the Moors are clearly desert tents. Set low against the ground with an easy slope to the roof, they are designed to let the fierce desert winds slip over them. The tent is small compared to most black tents. There is no headroom except under the peak, and this space is taken up by the center poles. With few

MOOR

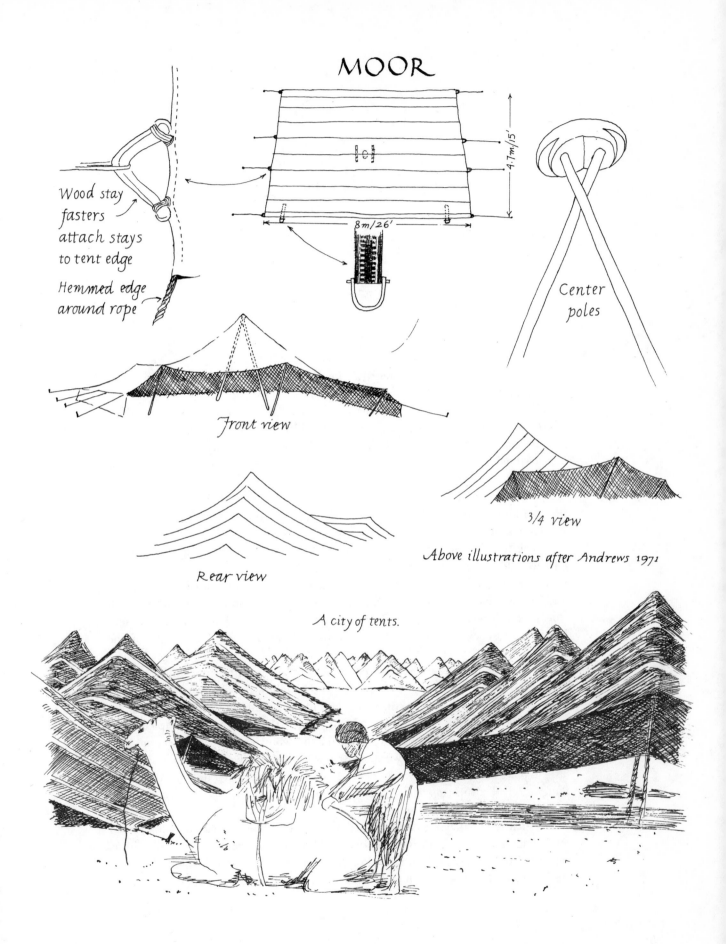

Wood stay fasters attach stays to tent edge

Hemmed edge around rope

4.7 m/15'

8 m/26'

Center poles

Front view

Rear view

3/4 view

Above illustrations after Andrews 1971

A city of tents.

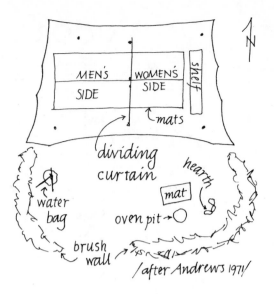

Men's Side / Women's Side / shelf / mats / dividing curtain / hearth / mat / water bag / oven pit / brush wall / *after Andrews 1971*

poles or extra wall cloths, this tent can be pitched quickly even in a storm. More than in most black tents, the tent *is* the roof.

The cloth breadths of goat's hair are woven in two widths, a sixteen-inch width for the roof cloth and an eight-inch width for the front and rear edges. The narrow breadth acts as reinforcement of these edges. The seams of the tent are sewn with a light-colored yarn so that the stitching stands out from the cloth. The stitching near the peak is done in distinctive patterns which are unique to each individual tribe. New cloth breadths are added to the middle of the roof and are darker than the sun-bleached outer breadths, so that the tent is striped in shades of brown from almost black to cream.

The tent is held up by two center poles set into a short ridgepiece. Each narrow side of the tent has wooden stay fasteners sewn to it from which run rope stays of goat's hair tied to wooden stakes. (Today sisal is used for the ropes and iron is used for the stakes.) Narrow side cloths are pinned to each side with iron pins and weighted down on the bottom with stones. The front of the tent has iron rings sewn to it to receive poles with which to raise the front of the roof.

The floor of the tent is covered with mats of esparto grass, and rugs are spread out on top of these for sleeping. Leather pillows, tooled and colored, are used to lounge on in the daytime. Tent linings of white cotton cloth are hung up over the back wall for warmth and to lighten the interior. A complete canopy of this material is sometimes set up on the women's side as a sleeping tent for married couples or single women. At one end of the women's side a shelf of lashed poles is set on trestles and covered with beautifully decorated leather hangings. Rolled up rugs and blankets are placed on the shelf, and leather bags with food and utensils are kept under it.

When a tribal band camps together, the tents are placed in a line, each tent about forty feet from its neighbor—a distance sufficient to keep the flocks separated when they are brought close to the tent. In this the Moors follow the Arabs, since the Berbers pitch their tents in a circle.

The Moor tent differs markedly from other North African tents. It has the usual ridgepole, albeit a short one, and the double center poles, but the tension bands, found in all of the other black tents of the western zone, have disappeared. Evidently, the Moors discovered they could do without them, but in doing so they had to shift the main tension of the tent lengthwise instead of across the seams. This is precisely how the tents of the eastern zone are constructed. It is doubtful that the Moors obtained this idea from so distant a place; rather, this must be their own independent invention. In any case, this tent at the westernmost edge of black-tent territory is a convenient link to the next section—the Persian black tents.

PERSIAN BLACK TENTS

Black tents of the Persian type are of much simpler construction than those of the Arabs. The Persian tent cloth is simply a series of cloth breadths sewn side by side with no other reinforcement. The rope stays attach directly to the cloth. The poles are unelaborate, either simple straight poles or the T pole, with no carving or painting. The tent cloth itself is always black and even the wall curtains are undecorated. The nomads of the eastern zone have been conservatives in the area of tent design; for untold centuries they have stuck with a design that must have sheltered the earliest of black-tent dwellers.

It is important to remember that the main pull in the Persian tents is in the direction of the cloth breadths—lengthwise. If this pull was across the seams, it would pull them apart. The end ropes that do the pulling always attach to the seams. Thus, the seams themselves serve the same function as the tension bands of the Arab tent, taking the longitudinal stress of the rope stays.

THE NOMADS OF IRAN

One sixth of Iran's population is nomadic or seminomadic. These nomads are found scattered over all of Iran, but the largest and strongest tribes are found in the Zagros Mountains which extend from Turkey to the Persian Gulf. These mountain tribes have a natural stronghold that has kept them free of foreign domination for centuries. In the northern Zagros, the Kurds have fought off foreign invasions since Sumerian times. (The Kurds were promised a country of their own after World War I, but they remain partitioned between Turkey, Iraq, and Iran.)

South of Kurdistan dwell the Lurs, the Qashqai, and the Bakhtiari. All of these tribes are fiercely independent. The men are famous as fighters, and the population is counted as "rifles" rather than as "tents" as most nomads do.

Today the tribes have been disarmed and tribal power is broken. In the 1930s the Shah actually outlawed the use of the black tent and forbad migration in an attempt to crush the Lurs, the Bakhtiari, and the Qashqai. Flocks died and the people starved, for only by moving could they live. The Shah was forced to rescind his edict, and the nomads resumed their migrations, but it was

MID·EASTERN TRIBES

clear that the nomads would not be able to resist the central government with rifles any longer. The government now admits to an economic value in nomad flocks but is still intent on settling them. The migrations are now supervised by government officials.

The annual migrations of the tribes in spring and fall is a massive undertaking. The Lurs and the Kurds make separate migrations, but the Bakhtiari and the Qashqai each migrate as a unit since there is but a single pass through which to move and a short season in which to travel. The Bakhtiari migrate with fifty thousand people and a half million animals, taking eight weeks to travel two hundred miles. The hundred thousand Qashqai travel over three hundred miles in two months. These movements must be carefully orchestrated so that the flocks don't become hopelessly intertwined.

Before the move, the weakest animals are slaughtered, and on the last night there is a great feast with singing and dancing. Early the next day a signal is given. Stakes are pulled, the tents fall down, and in an hour and a half the camp is ready to move. The tribal leaders lead off with their families, followed by the thoroughbred horses. Next come the pack animals and the rest of the women and children. Babies travel in cradles strapped to their mother's back; young children are lashed atop the loads. The flocks of goats and sheep, driven by the men, come last.

The Bakhtiari and the Qashqai have to cross major rivers on their way, a dangerous undertaking as the rivers are swollen and swift in the spring. Men swim on top of inflated goatskins and coax livestock through the icy water. Women, children, and the goats (who won't swim) are ferried across on rafts made of many inflated goatskins lashed together with a platform of poles on top. It takes five days for five thousand Bakhtiari to cross the Karun River with all of their animals and possessions.

When the mountains are reached there is still snow in the passes. Grass is cut to feed the animals on the way through grassless areas. A team of men go first and shovel a path. Then the tribe begins its climb up through the snow.

MOVING

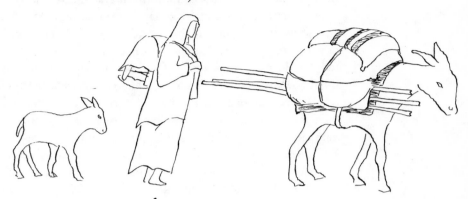

Women walk with cradles on their backs, the tent rides on donkey back.

Lur, Kurd, Bakhtiari, Qashqai, Basseri —
these and other tribes migrate in a similar
pattern & use similar methods of transport—
horses, donkeys & camels. River crossings &
mountain passes present major obstacles.

Women, children & goats must be ferried
across the river on goatskin rafts.

Men swim across on inflated goatskins &
herd the animals across the icy-cold rivers.

To climb the mountains
in the spring, a trail must
be dug through the snow-filled passes.

Tents and sacks become wet in the soggy snow and terribly heavy, but once over the pass the nomads descend into lush, grass-filled valleys. The thin, half-starved animals settle down and feast. During the summer the flocks build up strength and grow their wool and hair, and in the fall the nomads retrace their steps down to the plateau. Fall pasture is poor and there is competition with settled folk for these lands. Nomads often contract with farmers to graze their flocks on the fallow fields—for which the farmer gets his fields fertilized.

Every mountain tribe has a larger sedentary population than a nomadic one, but even the settled people are proud of their nomadic roots. Proportions vary depending on conditions: A nomad who loses his flocks may be forced to settle while a sedentary whose flocks increase may become a nomad. With government pressure to settle, the number of nomads is declining.

Like the mountain nomads of North Africa, many of the Iranian nomads are transhumants who spend part of the year in a stone house. The transhumants of Luristan follow a regular cycle in which three types of shelter are used. During the winter they live in a stone-walled house with a roof of thatch or tent cloth. In April they move up to the mountains and live under a black tent until the hottest part of the summer when they move out of the tent and live in an open structure of poles and leafy branches which is cooler than the tent. Then in the fall, they move back to the house. Increasingly, the transhumants are giving up the tent altogether. The flocks are sent to the mountains with a few shepherds who sleep in the open.

THE BLACK TENTS OF IRAN

The black tents of Iran are made of pure goat's hair, as are the ropes. The tents are usually made in two sections to keep the weight to within a donkey load. Each half has a narrow band with loops sewn along the edge to receive toggles and a large loop sewn at each end to which the ropes are tied. The loops are sewn into this band in a fan shape to spread the stress, as it is along this line that the major tension of the tent is taken. The frame used in these tents consists of either straight or T-shaped center poles supplemented by shorter straight poles set along the roof's edge. Both types of center poles are set under the ridge line where the two halves of the tent are joined.

The tents of the mountain tribes of Iran are quite similar to each other in construction. However, they appear very different from one another because the internal framework differs and the tents are pitched in a variety of ways. Thus, the peaked-roof Kurd tent looks very different from the wavy-ridge-line roof of the Lur, Bakhtiari, and Qashqai tents, but this is only because the Kurds use straight center poles while the others use T-shaped center poles.

It is even misleading to assign a particular tent design to a particular tribe, as the two types—T pole and straight pole—do not always coincide with tribal boundaries. To add to this confusion, the same tent may be pitched several different ways during different times of the year: When migrating, the nomads set up the tent cloth as a windbreak, which really isn't a tent at all; the summer tent looks like a box with no roof; and the winter tent has a high-pitched roof. This has led some travelers in the area to conclude that there are no identifiable patterns or form to these tents.

KURD

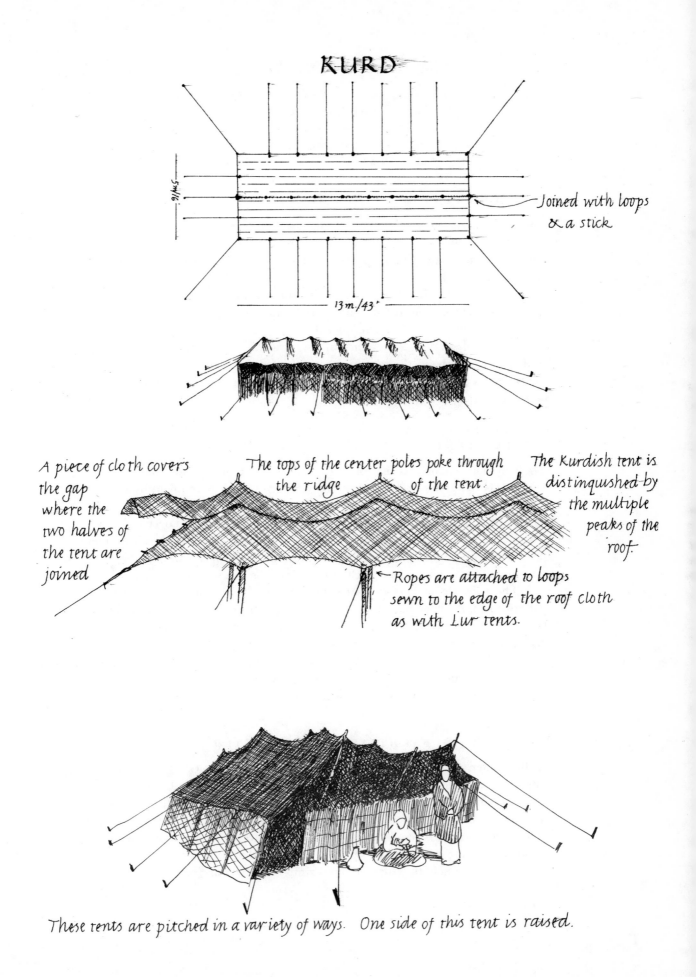

Joined with loops & a stick

5 m./16'

13 m./43'

A piece of cloth covers the gap where the two halves of the tent are joined

The tops of the center poles poke through the ridge of the tent.

The Kurdish tent is distinguished by the multiple peaks of the roof.

Ropes are attached to loops sewn to the edge of the roof cloth as with Lur tents.

These tents are pitched in a variety of ways. One side of this tent is raised.

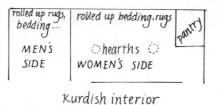

Kurdish interior

THE KURD TENT

The Kurd black tent is distinguished by its multiple peaks with its center poles that protrude slightly beyond the tent cloth. The roof looks like a miniature mountain range with spirelike peaks; the tents appear to imitate the mountains in which they reside.

The size of the Kurd tent varies with the importance of the family. Tents of the tribal chiefs (like the one illustrated) are often quite large. These tents are always made in two sections joined down the ridge line with toggles and loops. Side poles are set under the rope stays at the edge of the roof. Walls of reed matting surround the tent and are used for the dividing curtain between the two sides of the tent. Woven curtains are pinned to the roof to fill the space between the mats and the roof edge.

THE LUR TENT

The tent cloth pictured is that of a tent collected for the Danish National Museum by C. G. Feilberg. It is made in two halves, with four breadths to each half and a narrow band with loops with which to join the two halves. The longest breadths are in the middle so that they hang down and cover the gable. The ridge is supported by a number—usually three—of T poles. The center poles are made in two parts for easier transport. Other poles are set along the sides and corners and are used to elevate a side of the tent when it is warm.

The walls are made of reed mats twined with dyed wool or hair in colorful patterns. In the winter, the mat walls may be plastered with mud to windproof them; low stone walls are often built and the tent pitched over them to keep out drafts. Since the transhumants who use the tent return to the same campsite, the same walls are used year after year. A fine campsite observed by Feilberg had, in addition to the walls, a double row of stones through which ran a spring, providing "running water" for the tent.

THE QASHQAI, BAKHTIARI, AND BASSERI TENT

In the winter, the Qashqai tent is set up with T center poles, giving it a high ridge to shed rain. ("We pray there will be rain to shed," the Qashqai says.) The sides are let down to the ground and only the two ends are left open. When migrating and moving about summer pasture, the tent is pitched with no center poles. The roof becomes flat and the tent appears to be a large black box. Qashqai tents are distinguished by their horseshoe-shaped stay fasteners and the slotted poles that hold the tent cloth ends aloft—stretched like bats' wings.

LUR

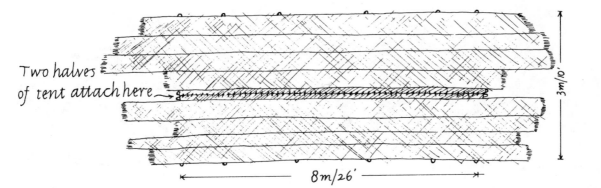

Two halves
of tent attach here

3 m/10'

8 m/26'

Loops on the reinforcing band & the
tent cloth are sewn so as to spread the stress.

The two halves of the
tent are attached by two
loops with a stick through one of them.

The characteristic ridge shape
of these tents is formed
by one or more T-
shaped poles.

3 m/10'

Reed mats with
designs in camel
hair are used
for the walls
of the tent.

1.2.0 m/14'

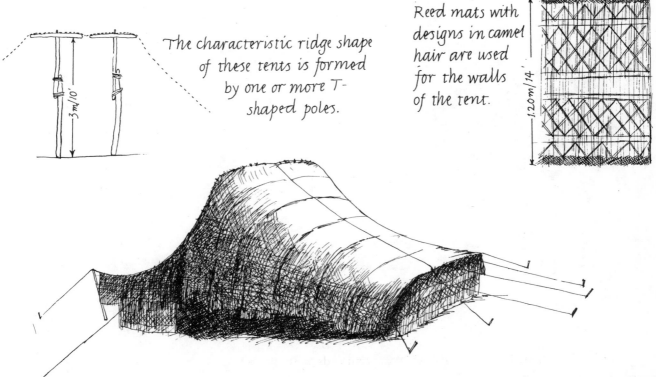

drawings after Feilberg

When migrating the tent is set up as a windbreak
& cover for the baggage.

QASHQAI

Among the Qashqai men pitch the tents.

Inside the tent the floor is covered with carpets. Large carpet bags filled with grain and household goods, spindle bags with yarn, and rolled up carpets are placed against the walls. Mattresses stuffed with partridge feathers are used for bedding in the tents of the wealthy. During the day, the bedding is rolled up and stacked against the rear wall. The hearth is set up just outside the tent in front of the women's side.

The Bakhtiari and the Basseri have tents very similar to those of the Qashqai. The Basseri winter tent uses four wall curtains while the summer tent uses only the roof cloth set up like a box. An average Qashqai tent measures 14 by 25 feet, a Basseri tent, 13 by 20 feet. The Basseri also use a mat tent.

THE BALUCHI

South of the mountain areas of Iran and Afghanistan dwell the Baluchi. Their homeland is Baluchistan, which falls within Iran, Afghanistan, and Pakistan. The Baluchi are desert nomads and live a life similar to the Bedouin. They migrate inland in the summer to the high country and down again in the fall to winter on the coastal plains. The Baluchi were once famous as raiders, covering great distances on horseback with a string of baggage camels in tow to carry the loot. With their raiding stopped, survival has become difficult because the countryside can barely support them on its natural resources alone.

THE BALUCHISTAN BARREL-VAULTED TENT

The Baluchistan barrel-vaulted tent was unknown as a distinctive variety of black tent until recently when two Danish ethnographers, Klaus Ferdinand and Lennart Edelberg, traveled to Baluchistan and made detailed studies of this design. Ferdinand concluded that this tent is the result of adapting the ancient arched hut for use with a black-tent cloth. The arched hut was once widespread over the whole of the Middle East, but was pushed aside by other house and tent forms. Survivals of this type are still found at the fringes of the black-tent zone (see Chapter Two). The barrel-vaulted black tent is also found among the Duranni Pushtuns and the Moghuls of Afghanistan.

The use of the barrel-vaulted frame for the black tent offers certain advantages. The hoops give the tent cloth something to rest on so that less tension is created in holding it up. The space under a semicylindrical shelter is more useful than that of ridge-roof dwellings. For this reason this design has been used for the lightest back-packing tents such as Stephensen's Warm-a-Lite tent.

BALUCH BARREL-VAULTED

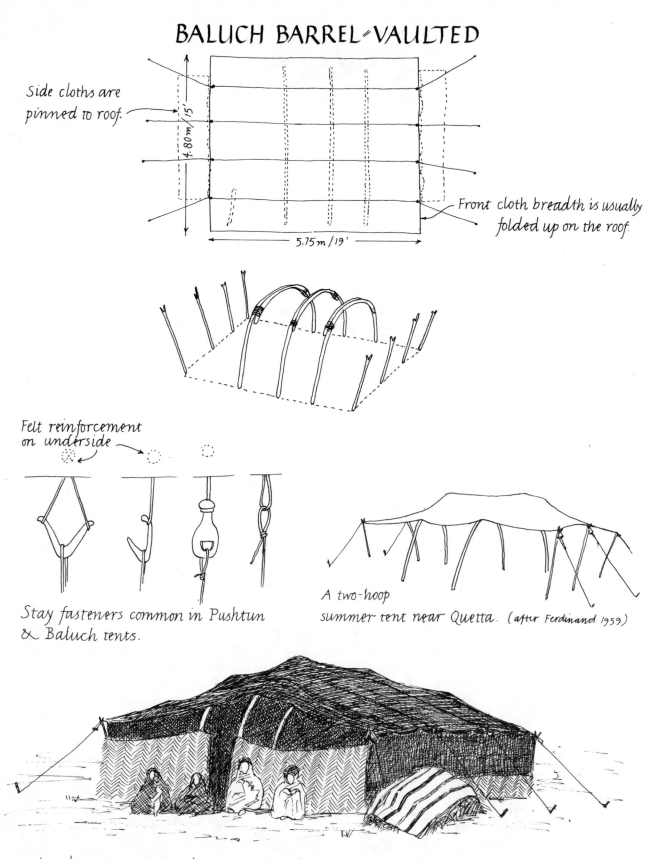

Side cloths are pinned to roof.

4.80 m / 15'

Front cloth breadth is usually folded up on the roof.

5.75 m / 19'

Felt reinforcement on underside

Stay fasteners common in Pushtun & Baluch tents.

A two-hoop summer tent near Quetta. (after Ferdinand 1959)

A three-hoop winter tent with clay-lined reed mats.   So. Afghanistan (after L. Edelberg photo - Ferdinand '59).

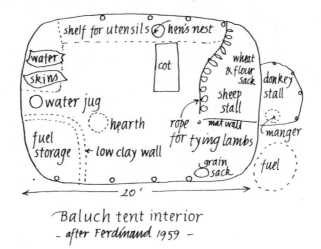

Baluch tent interior
— after Ferdinand 1959 —

The cloth for the Baluchi tent is made of goat hair in widths of about a meter. Five breadths are used for the average tent—three to cover the roof and one each for the walls. At either end, wall cloths are pinned to the roof; these are often rags or old tent cloths. At each seam line a rope loop is sewn with a piece of felt as reinforcement. The loops are attached to a variety of types of stay fasteners. The ends of the tent are usually held up by forked poles placed under these loops. The hoops that make up the frame are made of two pieces of bent wood that are lashed together when the tent is put up. The number of hoops varies with the size of the tent. In the winter, plaited mats plastered with straw are set up to keep out the wind and cold. These mats are attached to the stay fasteners. In spring plain mats are used, and in the summer the tent is left open.

THE AFGHANS

> In a turquoise twilight, crisp and chill,
> A kafila camped at the foot of the hill.
> Then blue smoke-haze of the cooking rose,
> And the picketed ponies, shag and wild,
> Strained at their ropes as the feed was piled;
> And the bubbling camels beside the load
> Sprawled for a furlong adown the road;
>
> —RUDYARD KIPLING, from "The Ballad of the King's Jest"

Afghanistan is home to a bewildering array of peoples. Through free movement or through government "persuasion," the tribal territories have changed many times over the centuries. Afghanistan is at the crossroads of the East, and influences are felt from Turkey, Arabia, Iran, India, and Central Asia.

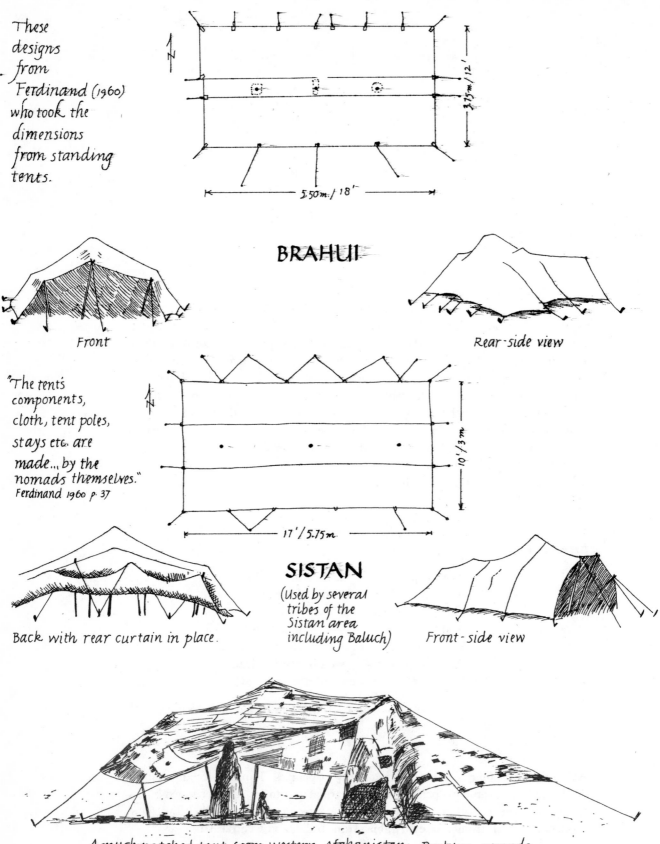

These designs from Ferdinand (1960) who took the dimensions from standing tents.

3.75 m / 12'

5.50 m. / 18'

BRAHUI

Front

Rear-side view

"The tent's components, cloth, tent poles, stays etc. are made... by the nomads themselves."
Ferdinand 1960 p. 37

10' / 3 m

17' / 5.75 m

SISTAN

(Used by several tribes of the Sistan area including Baluch)

Back with rear curtain in place.

Front-side view

A much patched tent from western Afghanistan. Pushtun nomads.

The principal black-tent nomads of Afghanistan are the Pushtun, which are composed of two tribal divisions, the Ghilzai to the north and east, and the Durrani to the south and west. One large Ghilzai group summers in the mountains and winters in Pakistan . . . or did until the border was closed in 1961 and most nomads were forced to winter in Afghanistan. In the past, this group controlled the Khyber Pass, the link between India and Central Asia. This became an important source of revenue for the nomads, whether through trade, protection money, or plunder. Many nomads lived in areas too sparse to sustain them but made up the difference through trade or caravaneering. Camel caravans used to travel down to the Indus Valley and exchange skins, wool, and rugs for sugar, tea, textiles, and factory goods. These caravans are presently being eliminated by truck transport as Afghanistan roads become paved.

Another Ghilzai group used to live in Central Afghanistan, but was forcibly moved north of the Hindu Kush mountains in 1890. These people summer in the mountains and winter farther north on the plains of the Amu Darya River. Their winter pastures are now being irrigated and settled by farmers. As with Cain and Abel, disputes arise between farmer and nomad, with the nomad usually the loser since the central government backs the farmer. But most nomads have very symbiotic relations with the farmers whereby the nomad winters his flocks on fallow fields to fertilize them.

Migration in Afghanistan may cover only a few miles (in the case of some seminomads) or involve the entire country. One Ghilzai group travels 250 miles to northern Afghanistan in the spring and back the same distance in the fall. This group, numbering ninety people, travels with fifty camels, twelve donkeys, five horses and six hundred fat-tailed sheep.

The nomads pitch their tents facing south in long irregular lines. (A few tribes pitch their tents in a square or circle with the entrances facing inward.) Women do all the work of pitching the tents, loading and unloading camels and donkeys, churning butter and cooking, and weaving. Men watch the herds but otherwise do very little but sit around camp and talk.

With governmental pressure to settle, many nomads now farm at least part of the year. They become transhumants who plant in the spring and leave for the mountains with their flocks and live in tents. In the fall they return, harvest, and then winter in mud houses. Even people who do not migrate may pitch a tent in the summer because the houses become flea-infested.

THE BLACK TENTS OF AFGHANISTAN

Since Afghanistan is at the crossroads of so many different nomad cultures, it is not suprising that it has many different types of tents. Here the black tent meets the yurt. The Hindu Kush mountains, running across the country from east to west, form a natural barrier between the two tent zones. However, there is some overlap, and black tents are found all the way to the Soviet border. Perhaps the most interesting shelter found in this area are the great variety of semipermanent dwellings, such as the yurtlike *chapari*. The line between the tent and the hut cannot be simply drawn in Afghanistan, as the tent is often in the process of becoming a house as the nomads become settled: Rock walls are built outside the tent to keep the weather out. If the nomad doesn't move for a season, he adds to the walls; with time the rock walls have replaced the cloth walls and the tent cloth is only the roof. Finally, the cloth is taken down, a permanent roof is built . . . and the nomad moves no more.

There are four types of black tent found in Afghanistan: 1) The Ghilzai straight-pole type, 2) the Durrani barrel-vaulted type, 3) the Baluch barrel-vaulted type, and 4) the Taimani semipermanent tent. The tent cloth for all of these types is quite similar; it is woven of pure goat hair in fairly wide widths of a meter or more. Some tents use a narrow breadth down the center, which functions as a sort of tension band since the center poles are set under it. It is common nowadays to see tents that are so patched that the original cloth is all but gone.

THE GHILZAI TENT

The Ghilzai tent is pitched with three parallel rows of straight poles under the roof. The center row of poles is high, giving the roof a moderate pitch with the outer edges of the roof cloth pulled almost to the ground. (The shape is something like the gambrel roof used on so many North American barns.) A small

GHILZAI

Ghilzai tents have 3 rows of poles which make a series of small peaks in the tent cloth.

DURRANI

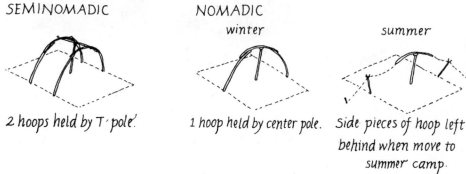

SEMISEDENTARY SEMINOMADIC NOMADIC

winter summer

5 hoops stuck in ground. 2 hoops held by T pole. 1 hoop held by center pole. Side pieces of hoop left behind when move to summer camp.

The Durrani tent uses less frame as it becomes more nomadic. A demonstration of how many nomadic designs may have developed out of sedentary structures?

Pictures & info adapted from Ferdinand 1959.

Nomad summer tent pitched.

wooden shoe or bunch of rags is set on top of the center poles to prevent them from pushing through the cloth. The front and the back are left open in the summer, but are closed in the winter with curtains pinned to the tent roof.

THE DURRANI TENT

In its numerous forms, the Durrani tent conveniently illustrates the evolution of a permanent dwelling into a nomadic tent. Many other tents must have evolved in similar fashion, but the various steps of the process are usually missing. In the Durrani tent we have these steps extant.

The cover is always the same goat-hair cloth, but the type of frame used varies depending on the season of the year and how nomadic the tent dwellers are. Semisedentary Durrani use a tent frame of five hoops made of reed bundles. (In Iraq the Marsh Arabs construct their great reed-mat houses in this way, and the Sahara-dwelling Tuareg also use reed arches in their skin tents.) The frame is always left in place and only the cover moved. A second type is used by seminomads. It uses a double arch of bent branches held up by a T center pole. The true Durrani nomads use two more types: a winter tent frame with a T pole serving as the middle element of an arch, and a summer tent frame that uses the T center pole alone. Thus, from a complicated frame of multiple arches we have moved to a frame of utmost simplicity.

THE TAIMANI TENT

The Taimani *arabi* is not really a true black tent since the frame is self-supporting. However, since it illustrates a semipermanent phase of the black tent I include it here.

The frame of the arabi is made of willow poles driven into the ground at two-foot intervals to form a rectangle about ten feet by twenty feet, with walls six feet high. A row of high center poles run down the center of the rectangle and hold aloft a long ridgepole. Rafters are added to this framework running from the wall poles to the ridge. The goat-hair tent cloth is thrown over this frame to form a gable roof of moderate pitch with vertical walls. Reed mats are often placed over the cloth walls. These long tents often house joint families of several brothers, a common practice among the Taimani. The tents are pitched on fallow fields in the winter so that the flocks will fertilize them.

All of black-tent territory is continuous except for the area between Afghanistan and Tibet. Here the western Himalayas cut across the territory and create a divide. This divide applies not only to the tent, but also to the culture; Tibetan culture is quite different from that of the other Persian black-tent peoples.

TIBETAN NOMADS

Tibet is home to a particular kind of nomadism that takes place only at high altitudes. The lower reaches of the Tibetan nomad zone run into settled agriculture, while at the upper limits vegetation disappears altogether. Like all nomadic areas, it is arid, but because of the altitude is subject to sharp extremes of cold and wind. That nomadism is possible at all is due to a single animal, the yak. This hearty beast thrives at heights and in cold where other animals barely survive. The yak carries the nomads and their belongings over the mountains and provides them with hair to make their tents as well as milk and meat. And the yak makes it possible to bring other animals—the sheep, horses, and cattle—to the highland pastures: A herd of yaks is driven through the snow-filled passes in the spring to make a road for the other stock. A typical nomad will have forty or fifty yaks and cattle, a hundred sheep, and a few horses.

The nomad camp consists of a circle of a dozen or so tents; if there is no room for a circle, they are strung out in a line along a mountain valley. Each camp is placed at least a mile from the next so that the herds won't mix. Winter camps are placed in protected valleys, but even so are often cut off from the rest of the world by the snow. During the six months or more of winter, the nomads make and repair tents and gear and trade their surplus milk products and hides for grain and manufactured wares. Weak animals are killed and the meat is dried or frozen to tide over the nomads through the lean times.

Most Tibetan mountain villages have a group of transhumants who pasture herds in the mountains for the summer and live in tents. In the winter they return to the village to live in stone houses. Their herds have few yaks but many sheep, cattle, and goats. Some of these transhumants become seminomads and live the year around in tents, but they still retain links with the villages and so are not true nomads. However, occasionally these herders accumulate enough animals to join the nomad camps and leave settled life behind. In Tibet, movement has always been from sedentary to nomad, but with Chinese control, the nomads are being "persuaded" to settle and leave their herds in the care of herding brigades. True migratory nomadism is seen as being incompatible with the modern "worker's state."

THE TIBETAN BLACK TENT

The Tibetans call their yak-hair tent *ba-nag*—"black tent." It is a true black tent made of cloth breadths woven on a horizontal ground loom. Its manner of construction shows it to be related to the other black tents of the Eastern type: The cloth breadths run parallel to the ridgepole, and the two halves of the tent are joined down the middle with toggles and loops. Its boxlike appearance even recalls the summer tents of the Qashqai.

The tent cloth is made of yarn from the belly hair of the yak, which ideally should be pulled rather than cut so that the hairs are as long as possible. Spinning is done by both men and women. The women then weave narrow breadths of fabric a foot wide by thirty to thirty-six feet long, depending on the size of the tent. These breadths are sewn together by the men using yak-hair thread. The tent is made in two sections (each half makes a full yak load) and joined with loops and yak-horn toggles. A section of the middle two breadths is left out for the smoke hole which has long loops and toggles running across it to hold together the two sides of the tent. This smoke hole, which also serves as a skylight, is large—two feet wide and several feet long. It is covered with a flap of cloth in case of snow or rain.

A new tent is always made for each new family, for tents are not replaced but are renewed every year by adding two new cloth breadths on either side of the smoke hole. Though daylight can be seen through the weave of the tent cloth, the natural greasiness of the hair and the oily smoke of the yak dung burned inside soon render it waterproof.

The tent roof is held up by two vertical poles that support a ridgepole, which runs the length of the tent. There are travel tents that use these supports alone, but the family tents all rely on external ropes and poles to pull the roof out so that it is practically flat with the walls hanging vertically. The yak-hair ropes are attached to the corners and sides where the roof meets the walls and pass over external prop poles. These poles can be shifted in distance and angle

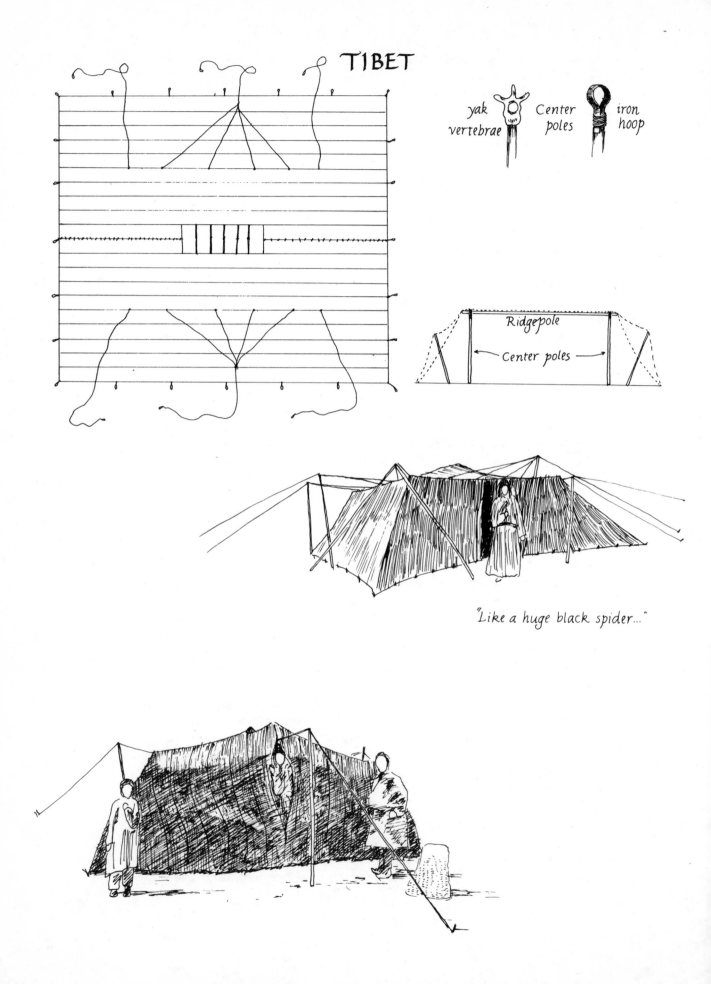

TIBET

yak vertebrae   Center poles   iron hoop

Ridgepole

← Center poles →

"Like a huge black spider..."

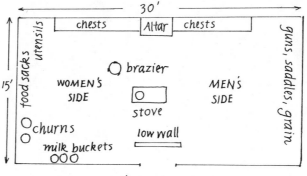

Tibetan interior

to give any desired pull on the tent roof, which is virtually hung between them. The side ropes are a unique Tibetan feature—they attach to the roof edge in three or four places and are braided together to form a single rope that passes over the prop poles. The pitched tent, with ropes and prop poles, resembles a huge black spider.

These tents vary considerably in size and shape. An average tent is ten to twelve feet long, while a large family tent may be fifteen feet wide by thirty feet long. A tent of thirty-eight by fifty-five feet has been recorded, and the Dalai Lama's tent was said to be able to hold three hundred people—which means it was even larger. Tents are sometimes connected at the ends to form one long tent. The shapes of all these tents may be square, rectangular, or even hexagonal, depending on how they are pitched. Mud or stone walls are built inside or outside the tent in winter to keep out drafts. In Eastern Tibet they are built four or five feet high as protection from brigands as well as the elements.

A fire pit is dug under the smoke hole and over this a mud or stone stove is constructed. Boxes and sacks filled with food and kitchen utensils are stacked against the wall on the women's side; on the men's side, saddles and other herding equipment are placed against the walls. At the end opposite the door is the altar where butter lamps illuminate a serene Buddha and other religious figures —the protectors of the tent and the family.

The black-tent zone meets the yurt zone in Tibet as it does in Afghanistan and Iran. Tibet, with its cold and windy climate, seems a likely country for the yurt and in fact, even the nomads that use only the black tent admit the yurt to be a better shelter for Tibetan weather. A few Tibetans under Mongol influence use the yurt, and the yurt is sometimes used as a temple among black-tent dwellers. But the yurt requires much wood and special woodworking skills not native to the Tibetans, and the ba-nag is considered the native tent while the yurt is a foreigner. As always, cultural considerations outweigh climactic ones.

CHAPTER TWO

THE MIDDLE EASTERN MAT-SKIN TENT

MAT, SKIN, AND BARK DWELLINGS

One might almost say that the domed hut is as specific to man, in a cultural sense, as the oriole's special kind of nest is instinctively specific to orioles.

—CARLETON COON, *The Hunting Peoples*

Simple stick frame dwellings covered with skin, bark, or mats are found over the whole world, particularly among hunting and gathering peoples. A ready supply of skins is one of the fruits of hunting, and most hunting peoples use these both for clothing and shelter. Where suitable bark can be obtained, it is also used; and wherever reeds, rushes, or long thin leaves grow, they are plaited or woven into mats both for floor and house cover.

These materials are, by their very nature, flexible and can be rolled up and moved; if the people using such a shelter are nomadic, it is a simple matter for them to move their house cover with them. When the cover is moved, the frame is often left behind. As long as frame materials are close at hand, it is easier to cut new frame poles than to carry the old ones along. But when the tent is used in wood-scarce territory, the frame must be moved also. Since it is pitched and taken down many times, the frame is lightened as much as possible, and systems evolve that make assemblage easier. With this process the hut becomes the tent.

Tuareg skin tent

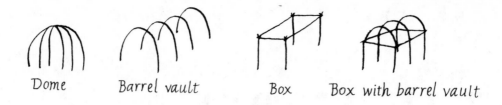

Dome   Barrel vault   Box   Box with barrel vault

Whether portable or not, these dwellings have one thing in common: the frame must be freestanding. It must hold up its own weight as well as that of the cover. Unlike the cloth used in the black tent, skin and mats have little tensile strength and cannot be greatly stretched. Thus, these tents must have more complex frames than those of the black tents.

The most commonly used frame for these tents (and huts) is a dome made of bent poles crossed over one another and lashed in place. The bent poles may also be set up parallel to one another to create a barrel-vaulted frame. A third type of frame uses straight poles to form a simple box. These three basic types may be combined in various ways; the box frame is frequently used with a barrel-vaulted roof.

The dome frame is not only the most commonly used frame for these dwellings, but is undoubtedly the oldest. The great masonry domes of both the East and the West can ultimately be traced back to the simple arched branch hut or tent. E. Baldwin Smith, in his study of the roots of domical architecture, put it this way: "Stone architecture the world over, from India to Stonehenge, began as an imitative and sculptural effort on the part of organized society to reproduce venerated forms which had formerly been constructed in more pliable materials . . . The most significant factor for this rapid assimilation of domical architecture was the existence among the Arab tribesmen, prior to their conquest of Syria and Palestine, of a native domical ideology, comparable to that of other primitive cultures, which had its origin in the religious use of an ancestral tent of round and domelike appearance." (*The Dome*, pp. 7, 42.)

At one time mat-and-skin tents were found over the whole of the Middle East, but with the Arab invasion these tents were replaced through most of this territory by the black tent. However, a few tribes at the fringes of black-tent territory continued to use mat-and-skin tents, and the mats themselves were sometimes kept as walls for the black tent as well as the yurt.

Mat-and-skin tents are found in a narrow band of territory that runs across the Middle East. This area begins in the Western Sahara and parallels the black tent eastward as far as Baluchistan, extending as far south as northern Kenya— almost to the equator. The border that separates these tents from the black tents usually follows tribal boundaries, but not always: among the Tuareg, a mat-skin tent people, the black tent is sometimes used; the Baluchi, a black-tent people, occasionally use the mat tent.

The southern border of the mat-skin tent territory is more difficult to define because the portable tent gradually becomes the stationary hut. The requirement that the structure be portable is somewhat arbitrary since some of the permanent huts are really as portable as the tents. Generally, the true tents are lighter in construction and more carefully designed than the huts. I will con-

MAT-TENT CONSTRUCTION

COVER

Dum palm leaves provide material for the mats.

Leaves are plaited into bands & sewn together into oval mats.

FRAME

Somali dome

Teda barrel vault

sider here only the most nomadic of these dwellings, those used by the camel nomads of the desert.

Mat-covered dwellings are still used throughout Africa and Asia. They are often the least expensive local housing since the materials are easily obtainable and can be quickly woven into large mats. An outstanding example still being used today is the arched mat houses of the Marsh Arabs of the Euphrates River delta of southern Iraq. Although these dwellings are not portable, they contain elements of both mat and black tents; namely, the reed arches, used by the Durrani in the black tents of Afghanistan and also in the mat tents of the Tuareg.

An interesting contemporary use of mats for semipermanent housing is seen in the *barridas* of Latin America. These squatter towns have no legal status, and since they are subject to eviction and destruction by the government, there is no reason to construct permanent housing. Thus, the barrida dweller makes his house walls of woven reed mats, which can be rolled up and moved in case of eviction.

MAT-SKIN TENT NOMADS

These are the sons of Ham, after their families, after their tongues, in their countries, and in their nations.

—GENESIS 10:20

The mat-and-skin-tent nomads of Africa are Hamites—descendants of Noah's son Ham. They are the original settlers of North Africa and dominated the area until the arrival of the Arabs, who converted them to Islam. In spite of this conversion, the Hamites clung tenaciously to their original ways. They retained their own languages, law code, and arts. Hamite women have always had more rights than their Arab sisters, possibly reflecting the matriarchal origin of Hamite culture. But most important, the Hamites kept their original dwellings of mats and skins, while other Islamic nomads converted to the black tent.

There are two branches of the Hamite peoples, the Northern and the Eastern. The Northern Hamites are Berbers. As we have seen, the mountain Berbers adopted the black tent, but the Berbers of the desert—the Tuareg and the Teda—retained their original dwellings. The Eastern Hamites, most of whom live in mat or skin tents, include a large number of tribes who dwell in the deserts of Egypt, Sudan, Ethiopia, and Somalia, among them the Beja, the Ad Sek, the Danakil, and the Somali.

All these nomads live very much like black-tent nomads. They inhabit the same type of desert environments; they herd the same animals—goats, sheep, camels, and donkeys; and, they live largely on the milk products of these herds. They even use goat hair for tent ropes, but not the tent itself. Why, then, did these people not adopt the black tent?

The answer is a cultural one. The Hamites resisted many facets of Arab culture, including the black tent. They were conservatives and stuck to their old way of life. Goatskin rather than goat hair was their tent cover as were the reeds and leaves they used for the mats. Although the mats for the tents and other articles are woven (or plaited), these cultures are not weaving cultures like those of the black tent. The mat or skin tent requires less time and is simpler to manufacture than the black tent; perhaps the Hamite women resisted the Semite idea that a woman's time should be given over to spinning and weaving. The Hamite women are excellent leather workers, as is often the case in hunting and gathering cultures. The Hamite nomads adopted a pastoral economy but retained the crafts that went with their hunting and gathering past.

NORTHERN HAMITES: THE TUAREG AND THE TEDA

The Tuareg and the Teda originally lived north of the Sahara with the other Berber tribes that dwell there today. During the great Bedouin invasion of the eleventh century, they retreated to the southern Sahara and settled there. In this harsh land they became camel nomads, noted for their great skill at training camels and for their endurance in crossing the desert with little food or water. Within a short time they came to dominate this portion of the Sahara, controlling the caravan trade that connected the North African coast with sub-Sahara Africa. These caravans became an imporant source of revenue, either through protection money or through raids. Until recently Tuareg salt caravans traveled 780 miles south to trade for millet which they brought back north.

Tuareg and Teda society is feudal in structure. There are separate noble, vassal, serf, and slave clans. The nobles do no work; they once spent their time raiding and protecting others from raids, but with central government control this has ended. Traditionally, only nobles could own camels, giving them control over all the other peoples within their territory, but this power is waning. Today vassals own camels and through education and positions in the new government bureaucracies are beginning to lord it over their former masters. The vassals do all the work of tending the herds while the serfs and slaves do the camp labor. The slaves are the descendants of black prisoners of war. They often do the work of tending gardens and palm groves in the oases owned by the nobles. These slaves may own property and there is a fictive kinship between master and slave; the slaves are now technically free, but often stay with their former masters since there is no other work available.

Tuareg and Teda women possess typical Berber independence—which has always upset their Arab neighbors. The woman's dowry includes the tent, the bed, and other tent furnishings, all of which she retains upon divorce (a woman may divorce her husband at will). The women of these tribes are unsurpassed as leather workers—they make the skin tents as well as the colorful bed cushions and saddle bags. Teda women are famous as fighters and wear daggers strapped to their arms with the handle down for quick draw.

Tuareg bag.

EASTERN HAMITES

Abundance and scarcity are never far apart; the rich and the poor frequent the same houses.

—SOMALI PROVERB

The Eastern Hamites inhabit the harsh and unusually barren deserts of the "Land of Cush"—Lower Egypt, Sudan, Ethiopia, and Somaliland. The nomads of the area are noted for their toughness and ferocity, an attitude they have cultivated in protecting their limited water and grazing areas—other tribes of the area avoid them. They are unexcelled at riding and managing camels; the camel is their standard of value, goats and sheep are "small change."

Because the vegetation is so sparse, the nomad's camps are small and far from each other. The Somali make their camps in a circle. At the center, a thorn bush corrals the sheep and goats; two to six tents are pitched around the corral and the whole camp is enclosed by a thorn fence to keep wild animals at bay. The women do the work of shepherding and prepare the meals of milk and millet. As among the Bedouin and the Tuareg, the camels are kept at another camp, often several days' distance from the family camp. The camel camp consists only of a circular fence in which the camels are kept at night. Boys are sent to this camp at an early age to learn the arts of camel husbandry and desert survival from the young men. They sleep in the open, live exclusively on camel's milk, and are toughened by these privations.

Of all the Hamites, the Beja have the longest history—they have lived near the Red Sea coast in the Nubian Desert for over 4,000 years (they are mentioned in early hieroglyphic texts). The Beja were once a powerful nation who fought the armies of the Pharaohs, the Romans, the Italians, and the British. The camel was known in Nubia by 500 B.C. and by the third century A.D., the Beja were harassing the Roman armies from camelback.

The Danakil (Afar) inhabit the Danakil Depression, one of the hottest places on earth. It is an area covered with lava fields and dried salt lakes—from which the Danakil mine salt. The Ethiopian government is currently attempting to settle the Danakil on newly irrigated land; the nomads are resisting, but recent droughts may force them to settle if they cannot replenish their flocks and herds.

Danakil camels of mat tents

DROUGHT AND CHANGE

First the soldiers came and took our swords. Then the trucks came; our camels were no match. Socialism claims our ancestral oasis lands. We have nothing but our freedom and our flocks. If we sacrifice them, our way is gone forever.

—A TUAREG TO THOMAS J. ABERCROMIE, *National Geographic*, August 1973

All nomads of the desert live a precarious existence close to the edge of thirst and starvation. In the past, droughts often decimated the nomads and their flocks and forced them to leave the desert, but when the rains returned the nomads always returned to the desert and rebuilt their flocks. However, the recent drought in the Sahel—the zone where the Sahara desert meets the savanna grassland—has been of a different nature. Some places did not have rain for seven years and in desperation the nomads cut brush for forage for their flocks; the sand moved in and covered the dead roots so that even when the rains returned nothing grew. But worse than this, the drought was accompanied by the Westernization of the Sahara which has resulted in new patterns of land and well use. This has upset the old balance between the nomad and the land, a balance that may never be re-established . . .

As with all nomads of the world, the old ways are eroding quickly among the Sahara desert nomads. Young men are leaving home to work in the oil fields and uranium mines; when they return they question the value of the traditional ways. Aluminum is replacing the clay pots used in the past; inner tubes are being used for water bags, and plastic for tent covers. Some of these changes might be for the good, but some of them are definitely not. Aluminum pots are light and don't break as do the clay ones, and inner tubes don't crack and leak as the traditional goatskins did, but the plastic tents offer none of the qualities of the skin or mat tents; they are unbearably hot and deteriorate quickly in the desert sun. But who can say how the nomads will fare? Perhaps their great ingenuity at surviving the desert will aid them in their new environment of oil wells, pipelines, cars, trucks, and government bureacrats.

THE TUAREG TENT

Tuareg tents were probably originally stationary structures. When the Tuareg became nomads they converted these mat-and-skin huts into portable tents, but they retained the frame structure which was too heavy for a truly portable dwelling. Thus, the frames are frequently left in place and only the mats are moved. The skin tents, on the other hand, have very simple frames. Some of them use elements borrowed from the old huts—the reed arches, for example— but others have abandoned the hut frame entirely and borrowed the T-centerpole frame of the black tent. The result of these combinations is a diversity of tent frames found nowhere else among a single tribe. Johannes Nicolaisen, who wrote the definitive study of Tuareg tents, catalogues twenty-nine different structural types—and this doesn't take into consideration the many individual variations. (These drawings are simplifications of Nicolaisen's work.)

MAT TENTS

The shape of the Tuareg mat tent is very close to that of the Moroccan Berber black tent. Although the materials used for these two tents are very different, it is no accident that these two Berber tents have the same form. This form is a very old one—originally used in sedentary mat-covered dwellings, later made portable, and still later adapted to the black tent. As is so often the case, the materials change but the shape resists these changes. The mat-tent cover (*asala*) is made of dum palm leaves which are plaited by hand into narrow strips of about a hand's width. These are sewn together with large needles to make an oval mat, several of which are used for the roof cover. The wall mats are different: They are made of straw or grass with leather weft strips woven in decorative patterns. Sometimes these straw mats are placed under the plaited mats of the roof, giving extra protection in case of rain.

The frame of the tent is made of very long acacia roots. To make the curved pieces for the arches, the roots are heated over a fire, bent, and held in position with ropes; when dry, they hold their shape and are then trued up with a knife. Most tribes make their own frames, but the curved pieces are sometimes bought from another tribe.

When the tent is to be pitched, a sandy spot is chosen and cleared of rocks and bushes. First the bed is set up; it is made of beautifully carved poles with a mat pad as a mattress (these beds are used everywhere in the south to keep the occupants free of insect pests). Close to the bed a forked pole stand is driven into the ground. This stand holds a food bowl out of reach of any animals that may wander into the tent.

With these furnishings in place, the tent is ready to be pitched. First, the curved pieces of the arches are lashed together and the three arches are stuck in the ground parallel to each other. Next, three vertical posts are driven into the ground at each end of the tent and a horizontal pole is lashed to these. Last, the thin rafters are bent across the arches and tied to the horizontal end poles. The mats are unrolled across the roof and around the walls and tied down—the tent is a home.

Mat tents are used by the seminomadic tribes of the savannah, who move only a few times a year, and by the true nomads, who move as often as once a week. When moving, the mats are used as a kind of pack saddle—rolled around the poles and suspended from either side of a donkey. Two donkeys are required to move the tent, bed, and all the household furnishings.

SKIN TENTS

Tuareg skin tents are made for the desert: The low, flat roofs can withstand any sandstorm. Even the color is close to that of desert sand, and the roof, with its gentle rolling curves, could be mistaken for a sand dune from a distance. But in-

TUAREG MAT TENTS

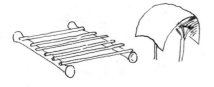

1. A space is cleared and the bed & a storage rack are set up.

2. Two curved poles are lashed together to make an arch. Three arches are put up, their ends slightly buried in the ground.

3. Three poles are set up in the front, another three to the rear. A cord is wound around the middle arch.

4. Horizonal sticks are put through loops on the middle arch & tied down at ends.

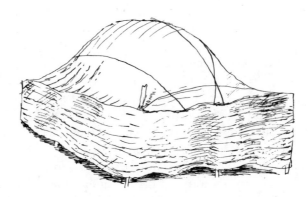

5 Palm mats are placed over framework & tied down.

side, the tent is another world: bits of colored leather and fringe hang down from the roof skins and flutter in the breeze so that the roof is in constant motion. Because of this quality, the Tuareg prefer the skin tent, even when it is not the most comfortable dwelling.

Skin tents are used by all Tuareg groups, although some use them very rarely. Among the northern tribes the skin tent is the only portable dwelling used. Skins for the cover are usually goatskin, although sheepskin is also common. The cattle-herding Tuareg of the Sudan have to use the skins of their cattle, but these are not really desirable since they shrink and harden when wet. To prepare the skins for the tent, they are dehaired and tanned; the tanning is poor, but sufficient for desert use. They are then waterproofed with butter and rubbed with red ochre and camel dung to produce a warm reddish yellow.

To make the tent cover, the edges of the skins are cut into rectangular shapes and sewn together using an awl with a leather strip as thread. A narrow welt strip is sewn into the seam which is cut into the fringe that hangs down inside the tent. The outer edges of the skins are left uncut so that the edge of the tent sheet has pieces of skin from legs or necks which serve as ties to the outer tent poles. The skins are sewn together in rows, the number of rows indicating the size of the tent; a small tent may have only three rows, while an average tent sheet of goatskins will contain thirty-five to forty skins and weigh about fifty pounds. A really large tent may have as many as 150 skins.

The tent frame is made of tamarisk wood—roots for the arches and branches and trunks for the posts and poles. The most common frame is made of three sets of three poles each. Each set consists of two uprights which support a horizontal pole. These sets are placed parallel to each other with the middle set made slightly higher to give the roof some pitch. There are a great number of other styles of frames. The Kel Geres of the Sudan use only a single T center pole in the middle of the tent with four lines attached to the ridgepole to hold the tent sheet aloft—the simplest Tuareg frame for skin tents and certainly the most portable. (The T center pole was borrowed from black-tent peoples—thus some of the diversity of Tuareg tents can be attributed to their capacity to absorb the inventions of other cultures, such as the Arabs.)

The central frame serves only to hold aloft the very middle of the tent sheet. Equally important are the side posts which are fairly thick and made in various heights from two to four feet tall. They are driven into the ground at the tent's perimeter and the tent sheet is stretched beween them; they combine the functions of both tent pole and stake. Traditionally there were always twelve of these posts, but this is not always followed today. When high winds are encountered, the tent sheet is tied to baggage or to stones.

In the past, the Tuareg pitched their tents facing west, but now follow Arab practice and face them south. When the tent is pitched, the floor is first cleared of rocks and brush and sprinkled with fine sand. The tent frame is erected and the side posts put in place. Then the tent sheet is stretched over the frame and lashed to the posts. The wall mats, made of reeds woven with leather strips, are then set up. These mats are often extended well out in front of the tent, making an enclosure courtyard that is an extension of the space inside the tent. The hearth is set in this space. The bed is set in the middle of the floor (in

TUAREG SKIN TENTS

⊓ BOX FRAME

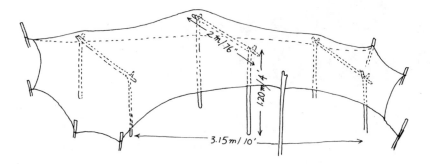

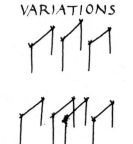

2m/76"

1.20m/4'

← 3.15 m / 10' →

A tent of the Kel Rela tribe. The frames for these come in a great number of versions – each tribal division favoring a particular one. To the right are some of the versions as collected by Nicolaisen.

⌒ ARCHED FRAME

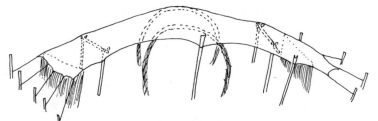

Another Kel Rela tent. This one has mats in the the ends. The two arches are made of palm fronds lashed together. The arches are usually placed in the other direction.

T" RIDGEPOLE FRAME

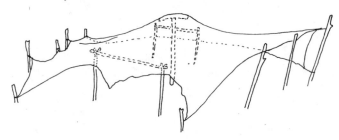

The most common tent form among the Northern Tuareg.

TUAREG · INSIDE

Every surface in the Tuareg tent is decorated. The roof seams are sewn with fringe and bits of of leather hanging down that flutter in the wind. The wall mats have patterns woven into them. The bed is carved to classic proportions and covered with incised designs. The cushions of leather have colorful patterns.

small tents it takes up most of the floor area). Camel saddles, saddlebags, and leather bags filled with grain and dates are set against the back wall. Just outside the tent are placed the wooden millet mortar and the stone quern for grinding grain, while the goatskin churn and water bags are suspended from tripods nearby.

The typical Tuareg camp consists of five or six tents placed in some inconspicuous spot out of sight of raiders or enemies. Camps are moved within two weeks at the latest as camp refuse becomes unbearable. During the hot summer months the tent is often stowed and the nomads move to the zariba—a hut of reeds, grass, or palm fronds—which is cooler than the tent.

Both the mat tent and the skin tent have their advantages and disadvantages. Mat tents take longer to erect than skin tents, but the skin tents are heavier and need additional posts at the sides to hold them up—an inconvenience. During the hot season, the mat tent is cooler—the higher cover permits air to circulate and at the same time the holes in the mats let the heat dissipate. But in the rainy season the mats leak and absorb water so that they have to be taken off and dried after each rain. Some Tuaregs combine the advantages of both types by placing a skin sheet over their mat tents during rainy season.

Thus, the choice of tent is determined by a variety of factors—heat, rain, availability of materials, and, finally, aesthetics. Some Tuaregs stay in their skin tents even when they are unbearably hot simply because they prefer the beauty of these tents over that of the mat tents. The familiar moving patterns of the roof above their heads—an upside down multi-colored leather forest in motion —make them feel at home.

THE TEDA TENT

The Teda tent bears a close resemblance to the Tuareg mat tent, and both must derive from a common ancestor. The Teda tent is more boxlike than the Tuareg tent—the walls are straight and the roof rafters have only the slightest

TEDA MAT TENT

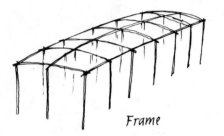

Frame

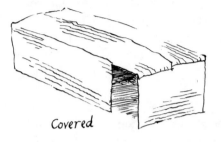

Covered

Interior : facing bed & wall hanging.

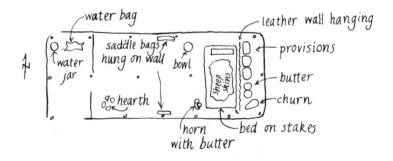

water bag

leather wall hanging

saddle bags
hung on wall

provisions

water
jar

bowl

butter

churn

hearth

Sheep
skins

horn
with butter

bed on stakes

curve. The frame is made by driving three parallel rows of forked poles into the ground to form a rectangle fifteen to twenty-five feet long by seven to ten feet wide. The middle row of poles is set slightly higher so that when the roof rafters are bent over them, the roof is given a slight curve. The palm-fiber mats are then rolled over the frame and tied down.

This tent is really a semiportable dwelling since the frame is often left in place and only the mats are moved to a new frame when the nomads move. During the rainy season the wall poles are slanted inward, giving the roof a rounded shape to shed the rain. The bed, which is placed at the end of the tent, is made in the same fashion as the tent frame—forked poles driven into the ground to support a horizontal pole. Mats are placed on top of these to support the bedding. A leather hanging of carefully worked colorful designs is placed next to the bed. This hanging is the focal point of the tent interior and is considered an indispensable part of the tent; it is the "jewel" of the bride's trousseau and is made by her mother and other female relatives.

EASTERN HAMITE TENTS

From huts of woven grass nestled under spreading acacia trees, administrators in patchwork battle garb run schools, clinics, plantations and prisoner-of-war camps. The huts are designed to be invisible from above, for in the "liberated zone" the Eritreans command everything but the airspace.

—THE NEW YORK TIMES, JULY 11, 1977

The tents of the Eastern Hamites are usually mat covered, but some use skins with or without mats. The frames are made of arches, either as a barrel-vault or as a dome. Except for the sheik's tent, these tents are generally quite small. Many do not have standing room. The roofs of these tents may be made waterproof so that they are better rain protection than the black tent, but the wall mats have an open weave to let the air blow through.

The Beja tent is related to the Tuareg and Teda tent in that it has a barrel-vaulted frame of three to five arches. The arches are usually supported by a ridgepole. In the summer, when the nomads are migrating, the tent is small and low; in the winter, when they seldom move, it is lofty and spacious. The frame is covered with five or more mats of dum palm leaves. The mats are smoked over a green-wood fire until impregnated with soot to waterproof and preserve them. The mats are stretched across the arches and tied to a row of stakes at either side of the tent. A low entrance is left at the east side of the tent.

South of Beja territory the most frequently encountered tent is the true dome covered with skins or mats. It is used by several tribes including the Danakil, the Somali, and the Rendille of Kenya. These domes are quite small—a typical Danakil tent is only four feet high at the center with a diameter of less than ten feet.

These tents are always owned by the women who also make and pitch

Beja tent

Beja tent Asswan, Egypt

Beja tent, Asswan, Eygpt

Sheik's tent ·Ad Scek tribe, Ethiopia.

them. The frame is made of thin poles bent in a half circle and lashed together with bark rope. A number of these arches are crossed over one another making a hemispherical frame. A single mat is wound around the walls and two more are set on the roof. The mats are made from palm leaves and are so compactly woven that they are waterproof. Cord is wound around the mats and branches. This frame is also used for skin tents and sometimes mats and skins are combined in the same tent.

When the tent is moved the arches are lashed together and tied on either side of a donkey so that the arches point skyward like great horns to make a platform on which are placed the rolled up mats and skins.

Inside the tent there are usually two beds—the left side is the man's, the right is the woman's. However, the men usually sleep outside the tent leaving it for the women and children. The beds are wood frame four posters with raw-hide filling on which sleeping mats are placed. Basket, carved wood, and pottery containers for grain, milk, and butter are placed around the walls. Two large water vessels stand on either side of the door. The hearth is located just outside the door. Often the roof cover near the door is extended outward to make an awning where the men sleep in its shade.

The Hamite nomads believe that evil Jinns haunt the fireplace, the threshold, and the rubbish heap. One must be careful around such places or illness will result. The Jinns are most active at sunrise and sunset, so fires are lit and prayers are said at this time.

If this book was organized according to types of tent rather than by geography and culture, it would be logical to proceed to a group of tents that are closely related to the mat-and-skin tents just described. The tents of the circumpolar zone (Chapters Four through Eight) are covered with skins (and occasionally with mats), and are close to the Middle Eastern tents in size and shape. The ways of life of the Middle Eastern nomads and the circumpolar nomads are very different, but they have this in common: Their lives demand a simply constructed shelter. Just about anyone can construct such shelter, and the materials are universally available—whether skins, mats, bark, canvas, or plastic.

The tent examined in the next chapter is just the opposite: Of all the tents in this book, the yurt is the most difficult to construct and usually village carpenters rather than nomads make the frame. But the complexities of yurt construction give it an elegance and form lacking in the simple mat, bark, and skin tents.

CHAPTER THREE

THE YURT

*The houses of the Mongols are circular and made of wands covered with felt.
These are carried along with them wheresoever they go, for the wands are so
strongly bound together and likewise so well combined that the frame can be
made light.*

—MARCO POLO

The yurt* is a tent that is almost a house; though it is as portable as any tent,
what tent boasts a doorframe and a wood paneled door? The shape of the yurt
is close to that of the dome, the dwelling form that encloses the maximum vol-
ume with a minimum of surface area. Outside, the winds slip easily around and
over this areodynamic shape. Inside, the circular walls and upward sloping roof
give to the interior a feeling of great space. The framework supports itself, no
poles stand inside, and no stakes are needed outside (an advantage when
pitching the yurt on frozen ground). The interior is kept warm in the coldest
weather by adding layers of thick wool felt to the walls; in the summer, the sides
can be rolled up to admit cooling breezes.

A yurt can be put up or taken down in less than an hour. Loaded on the
backs of two camels, bullocks, or yaks—one carries the cover, the other the
frame—it travels anywhere in steppe, desert, or mountain country. Because the
yurt frame is self-supporting, it can be moved without taking it down: To clean
house, the yurt is picked up and moved to a new spot. In the past, it was sometimes mounted on top of a wagon. Herodotus tells of Scythians who moved
their tents mounted on ox carts with axles twenty feet long.

Unlike so many tents that have all but disappeared in the face of indus-
trialization and westernization, the yurt is still in use. In the yurt's Mongolian
homeland, three quarters of the population still live in yurts, many of them factory produced. The capital city of Ulan Bator is surrounded by yurt suburbs. A
good yurt costs the average worker only two to three months' wages, and most

* The word "yurt" is Turkic for "dwelling." The Mongol word for the yurt is "ger," the Russian is "kabitka," and the Afghan "kherga" or "ooee."

Mongolian yurts now have stoves, electricity, and wooden floors. The yurt adapted easily to these conveniences: The stove sits in the center, the traditional hearth place; a stovepipe carries the smoke to the smoke hole which is covered with clear plastic to let in light and keep out the cold. In Afghanistan even settled people will often pitch a yurt next to their clay or stone house for the summer. When czarist Russia attempted to control the nomads of Turkestan, they built small castles for the tribal Khans to induce them to stay put. The Khans pitched their yurts nearby and used the buildings as cattle stalls.

YURT DWELLERS

Summer is like heaven, winter is like hell.

—KIRGIZ PROVERB

The yurt is found over an area that stretches from the Caspian Sea, along southern Russian, through Mongolia, and up into Siberia. This is the land of the great Central Asian Steppe, an area of little rainfall, fierce winds, and cold winters. Across this territory are spread Mongol- and Turkish-speaking nomads, descendants of the great Mongol Hordes who built an empire that stretched from China to Europe.

The key to this empire was the horse. The Mongols pushed horse travel and warfare to new heights; they invented the saddle and the technique of shooting from horseback with a short sinew-backed bow. "Civilized" nations were powerless against this combination; China built the Great Wall in a futile attempt to stem the nomad tide.

The horse is still the nomad's prized possession. It gives the steppe nomad the same freedom of movement that the camel gives his desert counterpart, and the horse became the basis for class in Mongolian society: the rich owned enormous herds, the poor owned none and were dependent on the rich. Heralded in folklore for its beauty, bravery, and faithfulness, the tough little Mongolian pony thrives on the steppe grasslands like no other animal. Even in the deep

winter snows he can forage for grass and, if necessary, can live on the roots of grasses. The Mongol's favorite drink is *kumiss*, fermented mare's milk.

The horse nomad's real survival, though, depends on great flocks of karakul (fat-tailed) sheep and goats that provide milk, meat, and wool for clothing and shelter. The sheep is the basic form of property; it is the unit of exchange that prices are quoted in. In addition, camels and yaks are kept for transport.

The steppe nomad survives by skillful herdsmanship of all these animals, each requiring a different pasture. He must shift camp as grazing land runs bare, but since each move means the loss of some animals on the march, he attempts to minimize each move. Because the pasture in any given area is limited, only a few yurt families camp together for most of the year, but in the winter a large tribal group comes together in some sheltered spot and awaits the spring. The yurt camp, or *aul*, is set up—like the yurt itself—in a circle with an opening, the "door," facing south.

The steppe tribes that dwell in yurts may be divided into two groups according to the type of yurt they use (this division was first proposed in 1896 by the Russian ethnographer Charusin). The *Mongol* or Kalmuck yurt is used by the Mongol, Altian, Buriat, and Tatar tribes of the east and the Kalmuck tribes of the west, most of which speak a Mongol-derived language. The yurt used by these peoples has straight roof poles making the roof a cone. The *Kirgiz* or Turkic yurt has a curve in the roof poles which makes the roof into a dome. It is used by the Turkic-speaking peoples to the west, the Kirgiz, Kazaks, Uzbeks, and Turkmen. In addition to the roof shape there are other characteristics that tend to go with each style which I will take up in the section on yurt construction.

YURT CONSTRUCTION

The yurt is unquestionably one of the greatest inventions Asia has brought forth. Its circular structure and dome-like roof combine the maximum structure with extraordinary stability. During my stay in the Pamirs the heaviest storms raged over the aul *without a moments cessation all through January, yet never once was one yurt blown down.*

—GUSTAV KRIST, *Alone Through the Forbidden Land*

The yurt and felt are both inventions of Central Asia. Feltmaking is an ancient craft (historically preceding spinning and weaving) and a simple process: Wool is fluffed, spread out on a reed mat, moistened, and rolled and beaten again and again until the fibers mat together. In Asia, felt is used for hats, outer garments, boots, and rugs, as well as a cover for dwellings. This material is unsurpassed as protection against cold, wind, and rain. As many as eight layers of felt may cover a yurt in the winter, and sometimes the top layer is oiled to help water run off. But felt has one deficiency—it has little tensile strength and can be easily pulled apart. Therefore, a felt-covered structure must be self-supporting; it cannot rely on the felt to hold up the poles as is done in black tents.

FELTMAKING

White felt is considered sacred by the Mongols.

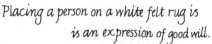

Placing a person on a white felt rug is is an expression of good will.

1. Wool is fluffed with light rods.

2. Water is sprinkled over the felt which is rolled up in a reed mat over a pole.

3. After soaking, the roll is pulled behind a yak or other animal.

4. The mat is unrolled, the felt separated from the reed mat & rolled under the forearm.

COVERING

The tradional yurt covering was always felt. Up to eight layers of felt may be used in the wintertime.

KIRGIZ ~ a design in brown felt is sewn to the border of the white felt cover.

MONGOL ~ A colored "collar" is placed on the roof.

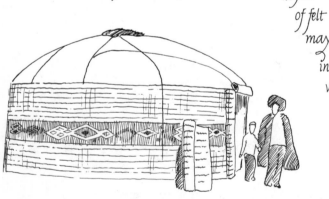

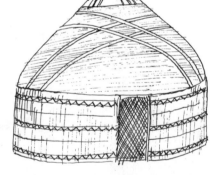

TURKMEN ~ reed mats on the wall with a woven band.

UZBEK ~ black felt roof with white bands. Reed mat walls.

CONTEMPORARY MONGOLIAN ~ canvas covered to protect the felt.

1. A white canvas is placed over roof.

2. Felt pieces on walls & roof.

3. Fitted canvas cover goes over felt & is tied down.

YURT CONSTRUCTION

THE WALLS

SLATS are // usually willow poles, debarked, split in half and crossed over one another.

HINGES

RAWHIDE — holes are bored, or burned, in the slats. A piece of wet rawhide is knotted at one end, pulled thru the holes and knotted at the other end. The rawhide dries, pulling the slats together.

SIMPLE LASHING used by Baluchi nomads of Iran.

KHANA (wall sections) are made by attaching 33 slats to each other.

MODERN
rivet
screw

The khana are lashed together.

FOLDED KHANA

EXPANDED KHANA

about 4 ft.

these overlap

THE FRAME

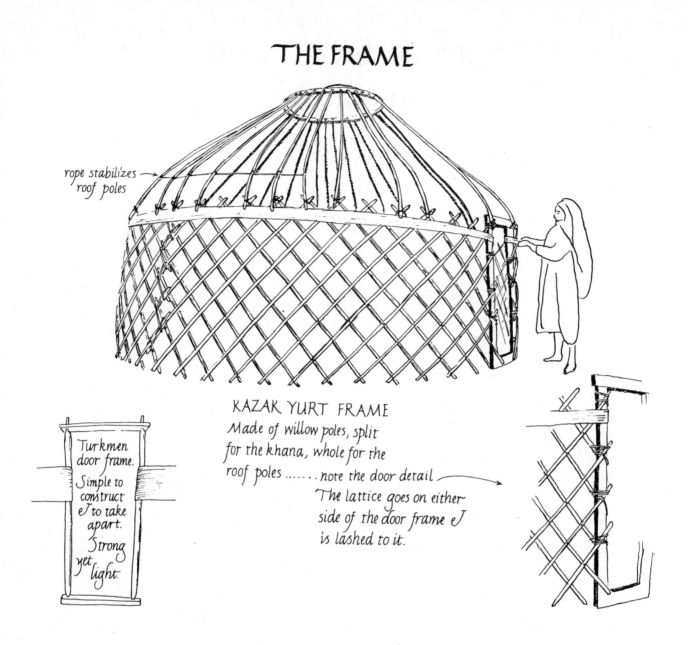

rope stabilizes roof poles

KAZAK YURT FRAME
Made of willow poles, split
for the khana, whole for the
roof poles .... note the door detail
The lattice goes on either
side of the door frame &
is lashed to it.

Turkmen door frame.
Simple to construct & to take apart. Strong yet light.

The yurt was created to provide a portable framework to support a felt-tent cover. In addition, the frame had to be made of materials found in wood-scarce regions where the poles are not large. One advantage of the yurt is that the frame does not use poles of any great diameter. Willow suits these requirements perfectly; it is tough and grows plentifully in the steppe areas. The wall sections of the yurt are made of willow rods an inch or less in diameter, split in half, and crisscrossed over one another with hinged joints of knotted rawhide. Not only does this make the walls portable, but the diagonal direction of the slats increase the strength and stability of the walls. A roof pole is tied at each crisscross at the top of the walls. At their top ends the roof poles socket into a bent circle of wood, the crown. A simple conical roof can be constructed of roof poles joined at the top, tipi style, but the crown allows for shorter roof poles and creates an unencumbered hole for smoke and light.

The roof and walls are now tied together but will not stand permanently. Left alone, the roof poles will push the wall sections back, unfolding them to the ground. For this reason, a woven band is tied around the top of the wall. This "tension band" is the keystone of the yurt; all the compressive forces that push outward are held inward by this band. Some yurt dwellers honor the function of this band by weaving it with intricate patterns that denote a particular family, clan, or tribe just as their rugs do.

THE MONGOL-KALMUCK YURT

A yurt is measured by the number of wall sections or *khana* it has. A typical family yurt in Mongolia has six or eight khanas which make a yurt of sixteen or twenty feet in diameter. A large ceremonial yurt described in the *National Geographic* (March 1962) used twenty-four khana and could seat "a hundred people comfortably."

The Mongol yurt commonly has a very heavy crown which must be supported by two upright posts. This crown is made of a circle of mortised and tenoned wood with eight or ten curved spokes attached to a central hub. The best Mongol yurts have a double set of paneled doors for weather protection. All of the doors, uprights, crown, and roof poles are painted with intricate colored designs. Factory yurts are plainer. Outside Mongolia most yurts use a simpler and lighter crown supported by the roof poles alone.

The finished yurt frame is covered. Traditionally the only covering was felt. Nowadays, a canvas sheet is first placed over the roof, then trapezoid-shaped pieces of felt are placed over this, and finally a canvas cover is pulled over both roof and walls and tied down. A felt or canvas smoke flap is pushed through the roof with poles and tied in place. This flap can be pulled from one side to the other as the wind changes direction, or it can be pulled completely over the smoke hole in case of rain. In the winter earth is sometimes thrown around the walls to block the wind, or low walls may be built of adobe or stone. Because of rain in the summer, a trench is dug around the yurt.

THE TURKIC-KIRGIZ YURT

Most yurts of the Kirgiz variety appear somewhat crude compared to the Mongol type, perhaps because these tents inhabit poorer regions. However, they are in no way inferior and dispense with the heavier crown and center poles of the Mongol yurt. In size these yurts vary widely depending on the tribe and wealth of the family. The small yurts of the poor may only be ten feet in diameter while those of the wealthy can be twenty feet or more. All of the wooden parts of these yurts use naturally shaped willow rods and saplings with a minimum of cutting and joinery. This gives these components superior strength because they are used whole or are split and not sawed (the saw always cuts across some grain weakening the wood).

The roof poles are cut green, soaked, debarked, and then heated at one end and bent to shape. The natural taper of the sapling makes a perfect roof pole, since the poles should be thinner toward the top for maximum strength

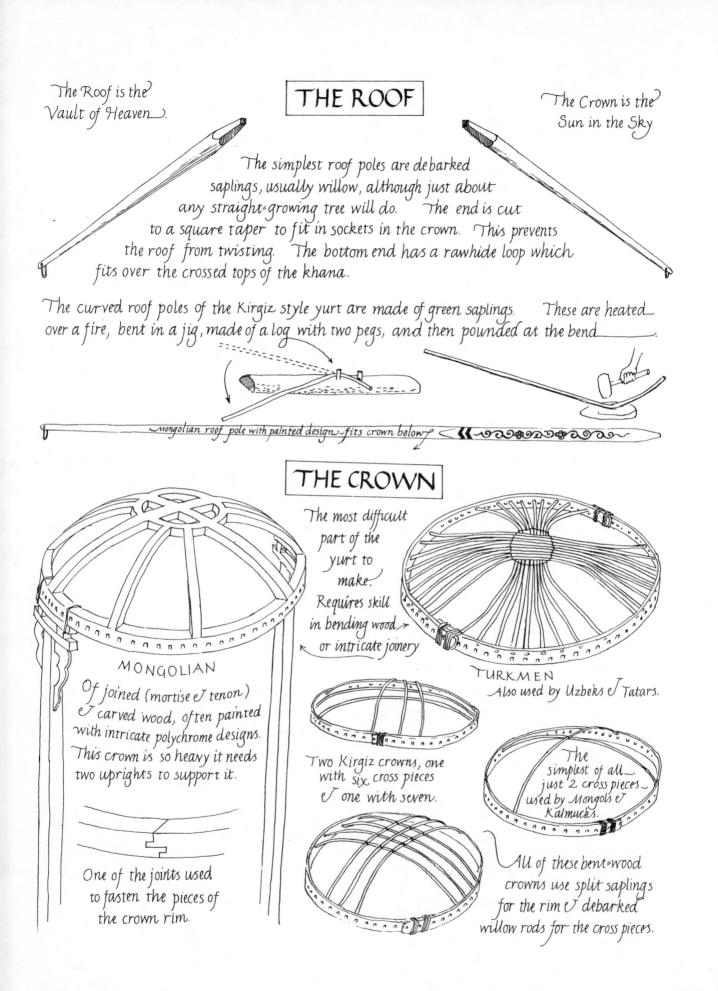

THE ROOF

The Roof is the Vault of Heaven.

The Crown is the Sun in the Sky

The simplest roof poles are debarked saplings, usually willow, although just about any straight-growing tree will do. The end is cut to a square taper to fit in sockets in the crown. This prevents the roof from twisting. The bottom end has a rawhide loop which fits over the crossed tops of the khana.

The curved roof poles of the Kirgiz style yurt are made of green saplings. These are heated over a fire, bent in a jig, made of a log with two pegs, and then pounded at the bend.

mongolian roof pole with painted design - fits crown below

THE CROWN

The most difficult part of the yurt to make. Requires skill in bending wood, or intricate joinery

MONGOLIAN

Of joined (mortise & tenon) & carved wood, often painted with intricate polychrome designs. This crown is so heavy it needs two uprights to support it.

One of the joints used to fasten the pieces of the crown rim.

TURKMEN

Also used by Uzbeks & Tatars.

Two Kirgiz crowns, one with six cross pieces & one with seven.

The simplest of all - just 2 cross pieces - used by Mongols & Kalmucks.

All of these bent-wood crowns use split saplings for the rim & debarked willow rods for the cross pieces.

YURT ENGINEERING

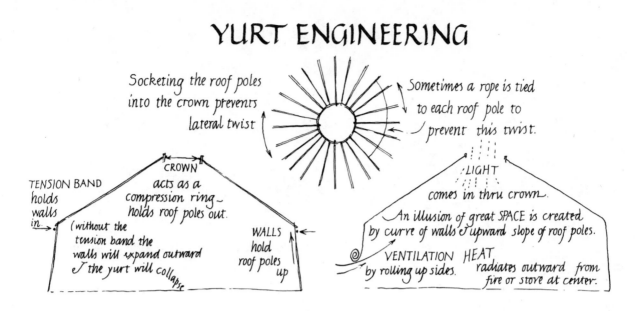

Socketing the roof poles into the crown prevents lateral twist

Sometimes a rope is tied to each roof pole to prevent this twist.

TENSION BAND holds walls in

CROWN acts as a compression ring — holds roof poles out.

(without the tension band the walls will expand outward & the yurt will collapse

WALLS hold roof poles up

LIGHT comes in thru crown.

An illusion of great SPACE is created by curve of walls & upward slope of roof poles.

VENTILATION by rolling up sides.

HEAT radiates outward from fire or stove at center.

and minimum weight. In some areas the poles are charred slightly to make them impervious to insects. In Afghanistan a yurt frame treated in this manner will last forty to fifty years. The crown is manufactured by bending two split saplings in a semicircle and fastening them together with rawhide or metal hoops. Across the crown are fastened wood rods bent in a concave curve to hold the smoke flap up. Each tribe has its own particular configuration of these rods; from inside the yurt they make a striking pattern against the sky.

The door frame is commonly made from juniper wood—light but tough and weather resistant. Many Kirgiz-style yurts have carved wooden doors (attached with rope hinges), but felt doors, which can be rolled up when not in use, are more common. Many yurts in the southern areas use reed mats for wall coverings—these afford privacy, keep out animals, and let air circulate in the summertime. In the wintertime felt is added under the mats and the wall mats may be plastered to make them windproof. The felt covering on these yurts often have felt applique designs sewn on the borders. The felt is bound to the tent with ropes and cords that cross the roof and walls in symmetrical patterns.

INSIDE THE YURT

As one enters a yurt it is considered impolite to step on the threshold or touch the tent ropes. The floor is covered with a thin felt rug in the summer. In the winter, a layer of felt is put down, then covered with four inches of dried grass, and topped with felt rugs. Today in Mongolia wooden floors are preferred—covered with felt and woven rugs. In the center a space is left for the hearth. Four boards form the hearth square and an iron tripod holds the cooking pots. Charcoal is burned where available, but more often there is only dried dung for fuel—the roof becomes blackened with its acrid smoke. Sometimes a stove was built of adobe with an iron plate top, but today sheet iron stoves are preferred.

PUTTING UP THE YURT

WALLS

1. Khana are expanded, lashed to each other and to the door frame.

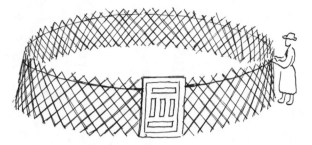

2. The tension band is placed around the top of the khana & tied to either side of the door frame.
This is why yurt walls slope slightly inward at the top.

ROOF

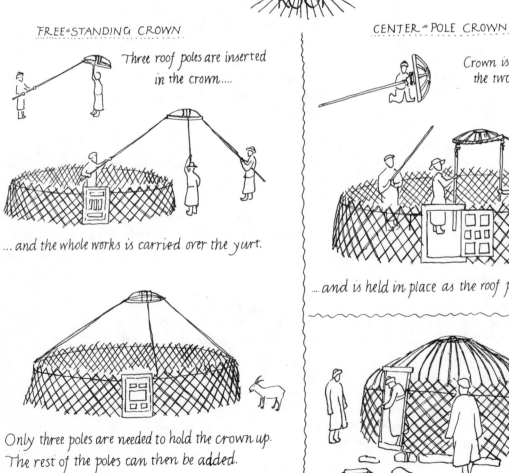

FREE-STANDING CROWN

Three roof poles are inserted in the crown....

... and the whole works is carried over the yurt.

Only three poles are needed to hold the crown up. The rest of the poles can then be added.

CENTER-POLE CROWN

Crown is lashed to the two center poles....

...and is held in place as the roof poles are put up.

THE DOOR

FELT DOORS

The original yurt door must have been felt. And felt still cannot be beaten for warmth & portability.

Kirgiz felt doors using brown felt applique over white felt.

Felt door with a "temple" doorway on a lama's yurt.

Felt covering used over a wooden door for warmth.

The elaborate paneling in this door was done by Chinese carpenters for a wealthy Mongol.

WOODEN DOORS

A later addition to the yurt. The yurt-owners main status symbol.

Uzbek double door

Mongolian paneled.

Mongolian yurts often have a single door outside & a set of double doors on the inside.

INTERIOR

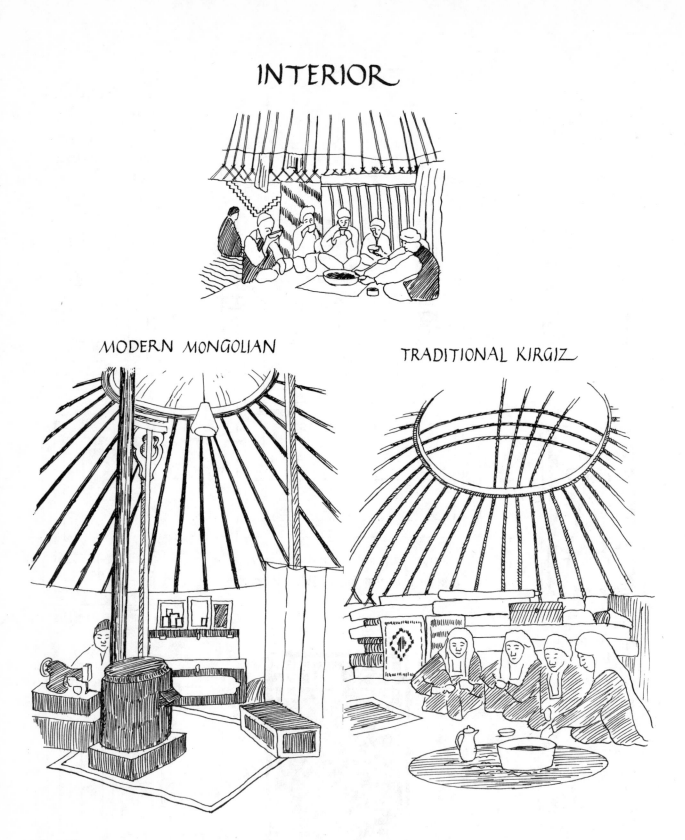

MODERN MONGOLIAN

TRADITIONAL KIRGIZ

The yurt adapted easily to modern conveniences. The stove is placed where the hearth once sat and the electric light shines below the skylight at night. The traditional altar place has family photographs.

Kirgiz women in the native dress, cook over a dung fire. Felt rugs cover all the floor except for the hearth. Rolled up bedding and carpets are placed against the walls.

Everyone and everything in the yurt has its appointed place. There is a women's side and a men's side. There is a "place of honor," a spot on the men's side in back of the hearth~ away from the cold. The young and sometimes animal newborn sit close to the door. Saddles, guns, and ropes are placed on the men's side, while the churn, kitchen tools and the cradle sit on the women's side. The yurt is traditionally set up by women, although men may assist. A bride's dowry traditionally included a yurt. Traditional nomad hospitality required that anyone stopping outside a yurt would be welcomed in for a meal. A lamb or sheep would be killed and there would be a feast.

Turkmen Water Jug

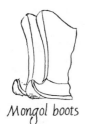

Mongol boots

Tripod for pots

Sieve of willow & rawhide

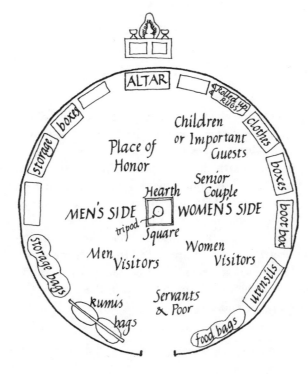

Kumis bag

Tea pot

Wooden bowl

Coal tongs

Kirgiz saddle

Churn

ALTAR

Place of Honor

Children or Important Guests

storage boxes

rolled up rugs

clothes

boxes

boot box

Senior Couple

Hearth

MEN'S SIDE   WOMEN'S SIDE

tripod   Square

Men Visitors

Women Visitors

storage bags

kumis bags

Servants & Poor

utensils

food bags

These have a stovepipe so that the smoke hole can be closed with a plastic sheet to keep the heat in.

The door always faces south or southeast, away from the prevailing winds. Opposite the doorway sits a chest that in pre-revolutionary times was the family shrine where Buddhist images sat with brass butter lamps and offering bowls. Nowadays, family photos and transistor radios have taken over this spot. Around the walls are placed chests, bags, and rolled up carpets. Decorative cloths hang from the walls and may be suspended as curtains to divide the yurt.

Everyone and everything in the yurt has its appointed place. The women's side is the eastern half of the yurt and the men's side—where visitors sit—is the western half. There is a place of honor—in the back of the hearth away from the cold. The young and animal newborn sit close to the doorway. Saddles, guns, and ropes are placed on the men's side while the churn, kitchen utensils, and the cradle sit on the women's side. The yurt is traditionally set up by the women although the men may assist. A bride's dowry usually includes a yurt for the new couple to live in. Traditional nomad hospitality requires that anyone stopping outside a yurt be welcomed inside for a meal. A lamb or sheep is killed and there is a feast.

YURT MICROCOSM

The tent is regarded as a sanctified shelter under the protection of which life proceeds. All clan deliberations and gatherings take place in the tent by which the Kirgiz swear: "I swear upon my tent."

—WALDEMAR JOCHELSON, *Peoples of Asiatic Russia*

Through the centuries, the yurt has become a sacred universe to its inhabitants. To the Mongols, the roof is the Sky, the hole in the roof the Sun—the Eye of Heaven through which comes the Light. And in the morning when one pours an offering on the hearth fire, the vapours mix with the smoke and rise up to God. The Buryats of Mongolia always keep their hearth fire burning—for the fire contains the house deity, the defender of the tent and family, which is handed down through the generations. No rubbish must be put in the fire, it must not be poked, and no outsider may take a light from it. For all yurt dwellers the hearth is a sacred area, the "square of the earth," and the five basic elements are contained therein: Earth on the floor, Wood in the frame enclosing the hearth, Fire in the hearth itself, Metal in the tripod over the fire, and Water in the kettle on the tripod.

YURT MICROCOSM

The tent is regarded as a sanctified shelter
under the protection of which life proceeds.
All clan deliberations and gatherings take
place in the tent by which the Kirgiz swear:
"I swear upon my tent." (Jochelson: Peoples of Asiatic Russia)
1928

"A man's tent is like a God's temple." Kirgiz proverb

With many hundreds of years of dwelling
in the yurt, it became a sacred universe
to its inhabitants. To the Mongols, the
roof is the Sky, the hole in the roof is the
Sun, the Eye of Heaven through which
comes the Light. And when in the
morning one pours an offering on the
hearth fire, the vapours mix with the
smoke and rise up to God. The hearth is
a sacred area, the "square of the earth",
and the Asian five basic elements are
contained therein: Earth on the floor,
Wood in the frame enclosing the hearth,
Fire in the hearth itself, Metal in the
grate over the fire, and Water in the
kettle on the grate.

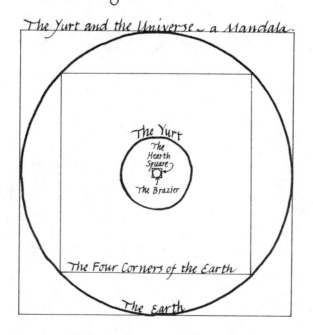

The Yurt and the Universe - a Mandala.

The Yurt

The Hearth Square

The Brazier

The Four Corners of the Earth

The Earth

THE VERSATILE YURT

Mongol yurt set for winter with a plank floor & earth heaped around the floor edge. Ropes serve as clotheslines; felt boots dry on the roof.

To air out the yurt, remove the cover, or pick up & move the frame. Note the stakes tied to this Uzbek yurt to keep it from blowing away.

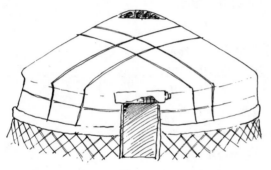

Summer — door & sides rolled up. Door is a reed mat covered with old felt.

The crown, a few roof poles & some felt are used as a temporary tent when traveling

Expanded khana used as a sheep fold.

Kirgiz yurt traveling by yak.

Turkmen yurt moving by ox and wagon.

YURT DERIVATIONS

The word YURT is a Turkic term meaning "dwelling", and accordingly, has been loosely applied to many varieties of habitation. In most cases, these dwellings (which are often quite different from the nomadic yurt) are a result of nomadic peoples becoming settled or sedentary peoples being influenced by nomadic design.

SIBERIA

Southern Siberia has (or had) many nomads who dwell in true yurts. The yurt's influence can be seen in these dwellings of 1) log & bark, 2) birch bark, & 3) bark.

AFGHANISTAN

The chapari is made by poor seminomads who cannot afford a yurt. Poles are driven into the ground in a circle to make the walls. Roof poles are lashed to these and at the top – tipi style. The cover is reed mats & old felts.

Buckminister Fuller's dymaxion house: "The Afghans regarded Fuller's geodesic as a Modern Mongolian yurt & consequently a native Afghan type of architecture." (The Dymaxion World of Buckminister Fuller)

NORTH AMERICA

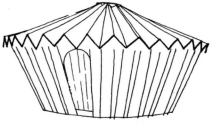

In searching for a house design that would be inexpensive & simple to construct, Bill Coperthwaite came upon a picture of the Mongolian yurt. After much experimentation, he developed the above Yurt. It is a wooden stationary structure, yet retains the basic principles of the nomadic yurt. Plans for a 17 ft. & a 32 ft. diameter concentric Yurt may be purchased by writing the designer at Bucks Harbor, Me. 04618

Two students of Coperthwaite, Chuck & Laurel Cox, built a portable yurt & have lived in it for 5 years in Alaska & New Hampshire. They have published a set of plans for this yurt. Write them at The Meeting School Rindge, New Hampshire, 03461

An early Coperthwaite design was close to the Mongol yurt, but used a lattice roof. Chuck Cox built a version which Len Charney patterned his yurt after & wrote up in Build a Yurt (Collier Books).

THE ALACHIGH OF THE SHAH SAVAN

From the outside, the tents of the Shah Savan look like dome-roofed yurts, but a look at their interiors reveals a difference: the crown and roof poles of a yurt are present but not the lattice walls. The Shah Savan have developed a "yurt" that dispenses with these walls. When traveling, it is not uncommon for yurt dwellers to make a temporary tent by using the crown and a few roof poles as a frame. At some time in the past, the Shah Savan must have modified this temporary shelter into their permanent home.

There are certain advantages to the *alachigh,* as the Shah Savan call their tent. It can encompass as large an area as the yurt with less use of wood—making it easier to transport. It is simpler to construct than the yurt, although the key element, the crown, is still the most difficult part to make. (The crown of either the yurt or alachigh is always made by specialists and not the nomads

SHAH SAVAN

The crown is held up & poles are inserted.

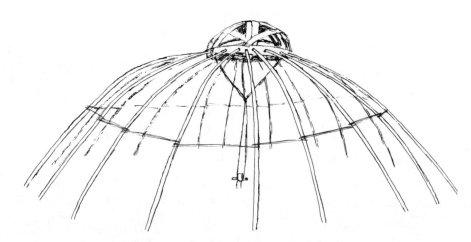

The frame is strengthened with wool bands wound around the poles.
A rope is attached to the crown which pulls it downward   to a stake in the middle.

themselves, and most nomads have all the frame parts made by carpenters who specialize in that craft.) The alachigh can be set up as quickly as the yurt, but does need a large center stake to hold it in place whereas the yurt needs no stakes at all.

The frame of the alachigh consists of the crown and a number of curved poles that fit into it. The number of poles varies with the size of the tent—24, 26, 28 or 32. To erect the frame, one man holds aloft the crown while others insert the poles. Brightly colored woven bands are then looped around the poles to strengthen the frame and prevent the bottom ends of the poles from slipping out. A band is tied around the crown, pulled down, and tied to a massive stake set in the center of the floor; this pushes the poles outward against the bands looped around them. The tensions created by this band system and the dome shape of the alachigh make it a very stable structure even in the highest winds.

The alachigh is covered with three large sheets of felt—one on each side of the doorway, not quite meeting in the back, and a third felt overlapping these at the back. Two pegs are set at the corners of the back felt, and ropes are tied from these and wound around the sides of the tent. Small felt sheets are used to fill in the rest of the roof and to cover the crown. Ropes are attached to the crown cover to adjust it according to wind direction. Along the very bottom of the wall rush mats circle the tent to keep out animals and afford privacy when the cover is raised.

Little is known about the Shah Savan. They originated when Shah Abbas (1587–1629) recruited an army from the best fighters of seven different Iranian tribes. In time these people became a tribe in itself. They live in the Azerbaijan Province of northwest Iran, wintering south of the Kuh-I-Savalan Mountain and migrating over it every spring to reach summer pasture near the Soviet border. They speak a Turkic language and follow the Turkic practice of counting their families as "fires" rather than as "tents," which is the Persian practice. Since the Turkic or Kirgiz-style yurt has a dome-shaped roof, it seems that the Shah Savan must have adapted their tent from this style.

The sides can be rolled up in the summer. The reed mats keep animals out.

The Shah Savan recently lost 100,000 acres of winter pasture land to a government irrigation project and the government is attempting to resettle them.

CHAPTER FOUR

SIBERIAN TENTS

SIBERIAN NOMADS

The southernmost region of Siberia is open steppe inhabited by yurt-dwelling nomads such as I have described in the previous chapter. North of the steppe, the country gradually becomes forested; the open plains give way to a dense coniferous forest—the great Siberian taiga. It is a harsh land, marshy and mosquito infested in the summer, frozen and snow blown in the winter. North of the taiga the trees thin out and then disappear altogether giving way to the tundra—a low, swampy plain where the ground is perpetually frozen except during the summer thaw which warms the ground a few feet deep.

The tundra and taiga of Siberia are part of the circumpolar zone. This zone, which circles the North Pole through Eurasia and North America should be seen as a whole. The plant and animal life and the human cultures found in this area are all related to one another. The taiga and the tundra are the home of the reindeer, who feed on reindeer moss, and home of the nomads, who feed on the reindeer. The reindeer and the caribou are really the same animal, taxonomically identical. The nomads who follow the deer have very similar ways of life to each other. Their religions of the Bear Cult and Shamanism are found throughout the entire zone. Most striking is the choice of dwelling, for the conical tent and the dome are found across the whole circumpolar area.

The reindeer is life itself to the northern Siberians. The skins are made into clothes, boots, and tent covers; the antlers are used for utensils, tools, and bows; the sinews are dried and pounded into thread; the bones are soaked in oil and burned for fuel; the bristly skin of the legs is used on ski bottoms (so that they slide forward easily but grip the snow and won't slide backward). Almost every part of the deer is eaten, even the head, the organs, and the bone marrow. Nothing is wasted. When the deer is killed the blood is drained into the stomach which is dried; the entrails are stuffed with tallow-like sausage; the milk is drunk fresh or made into cheese; the meat is dried for the lean times ahead. The body of the reindeer, when sacrificed to the gods, gives spiritual blessings to the nomads and their herds.

The reindeer was domesticated in Siberia about a thousand years ago. Reindeer were first tamed for use as decoys to lure wild deer to within shooting range. Later these deer were trained to pull sleds, and still later broken to the saddle and milked. With the introduction of the gun, the wild herds were exterminated and those who relied on hunting wild deer had to shift to herding. Migratory life—man following herds—became nomadic—man moving the herds. But this sequence of domestication was not followed by all peoples. The Koryak, who kept the largest herds, never rode their deer or milked them, and these most nomadic of all peoples kept deer that were the least domesticated and most unruly.

Not all Siberians lived by the reindeer. Those who inhabited the coasts depended on sea-mammal hunting; in the interior people lived by inland-water fishing. Most Siberian economies were a mixture of fishing, hunting, and herding. Those with small herds had to fish or hunt seal on the coasts and rivers. Those with large herds did little hunting or fishing. Like all nomad economies there was always some movement between nomad and sedentary. A nomad who lost his herd might become a fisherman, while the fisherman who put his excess wealth into reindeer might become a nomad.

THE KORYAK AND THE CHUKCHI

The nomadic Koryak and Chukchi are the high nomads of the north. They more than any other tribe in Siberia depend on the reindeer for their survival. Their herds may number ten thousand animals, and rich Koryaks have been known to have two or three herds this size. These herds have to be kept constantly moving as they quickly exhaust the moss pasture.

The deer are moved north in the summer and south in the winter. Winter herds are kept close to camp and moved as little as possible. In the spring the arrival of the newborn calves makes for a difficult time—families work day and night to find and protect the newborn. With the arrival of summer, the herds

Koryaks – from a painting by Geo. A. Frost

Ket sledge & driver

Nentsy tent-pole sledge

Evenks moving camp. Tent poles are suspended on either side of pack reindeer.

are moved to the mountain pastures of the north. Freight sleds are piled high with tents and baggage and hitched to the reindeer. Each sled has a line tied from it to a sled in front of it forming a great train. The men move out ahead and break trail while the women riding their special touring sleds follow with the children. The freight sleds and the herd follow these. Summer camps and their herds disperse widely to find fresh pasture, but in autumn all come together. It is festival time. Several tents are combined to make one enormous tent; days of feasting and dancing celebrate the meeting of the herd before the start of the great trek southward.

THE YUKAGHIR, EVENS, AND THE EVENKS

West of the Chukchi and Koryak dwell the Yukaghir, the Evens, and the Evenks. These tribes breed reindeer, but rely more on hunting, trapping, and fishing for food. The sedentary tribes net fish on the banks of the great Siberian rivers—the Amur, the Yenisey, the Lena, and the Kolyma. The nomadic tribes have small herds of reindeer which they use only to move camp. Herds are so small that families have to pool their animals when they move. The reindeer are left unwatched most of the year and rounded up only when they are needed to move. Some of these peoples use sleds, but more often the deer are ridden and used as pack animals. Some "foot nomads" have no deer at all and must pull their sleds by hand. Sleds are sometimes made by pouring water over skins and letting them freeze. In the summer, birch bark and dugout canoes are used for river travel.

Families winter in the forest and rely on trapping squirrels, ermine, and sable. Skis with fur bottoms are used for travel over the snow to hunt elk and wild reindeer. During rutting season decoy deer are set out with a strap in their antlers; wild deer fight them, become entangled, and thus fall prey to the hunters. With the arrival of spring, several households combine herds and move to high places for calving time. In the summer families gather at fishing spots on the rivers and pasture their herds together on the tundra. Smoky fires are lit to keep the mosquitoes and flies off the deer. In the fall the herds are divided, and families move off singly to winter campsites.

THE NENTSY AND NGANASAN

In northernmost Siberia dwell the Nentsy and the Nganasan. Their country borders Lapp country, and they share many traits that demonstrate their common origin. The country is quite barren and supports only a thinly scattered population; each family must be largely self-sufficient since the next tent may be fifty miles away. The herds are not large and deer are used mainly in the winter to haul sleds. Unlike most reindeer herders, the Nentsy and the Nganasan use dogs to herd the deer. Wild deer supply the mainstay of the diet, supplemented by other game and fish.

Winter camp is made in the forest or scrub tundra where the snow is soft and the deer can dig for moss. Herders make the rounds of the herd in a large circle driving stray deer back into the ring. In the spring, camps move north-

EVENK-YUKAGHIR CHORAMA-DYU

The walls are made of chora – a group of 3 sticks of equal length tied together at one end. Eight, 10, 12, or 14 chora are fastened together in a circle, leaving a space, front & back for entrance.

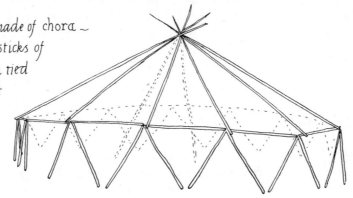

SIBERIAN GEODESICS:
the Chorama-dyu is similar to the yaranga of the Chukchi & Koryak but the frame is lighter & more regular in its construction.

The roof poles are held up by 4 poles at the center. A horizontal pole over the hearth supports the cauldron.

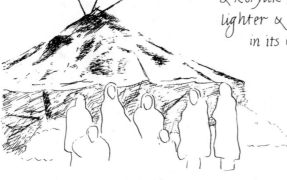

A group of Tundra Yukaghir outside their winter tent. Snow heaped around bottom edge insulates & keeps out drafts. The skin cover is of dressed skins unlike the Koryak & Chukchi who leave the hair on.

Putting up an Evenk Chorama-dyu.

Evenk summer tent of deerskin with birch-bark panels sewn to the wall covering.

ward, sometimes all the way to the Arctic coast. A large sled pulled by six or eight deer is used to move the camp, hauling the mother, the young, and all the family's possessions. Summer camps are made on river banks where fish are netted and dried for the winter. Families migrate separately for most of the year, except in the summer when the fish camps—with ten to twenty tents—are set up.

COMPOUND TENTS

The compound tent has a conical roof and a cylindrical wall. One such tent, the *yaranga,* is the largest tent (in everyday use) made by any nomadic people. Over thirty feet in diameter, it houses several families, all their possessions, and even a few dogs. This size is a reflection of the communal nature of these people, and is a testament to the engineering ingenuity of the nomads. They must construct this great monster of a tent from native materials capable of withstanding the most intense winds and snows found anywhere in the world.

These tents bear an obvious relation to the yurt. The shapes of both the yurt and compound tent are similar and their territories are adjacent to one another. The compound tent must be the predecessor of the true yurt for the frames of these tents contain the rudiments of the yurt frame. Compared to the yurt, the Siberian tents seem heavy and clumsy. Still, they serve their inhabitants well, and they have to withstand snow loads never encountered by the yurt, which may explain their unwieldy construction.

THE YARANGA

The frame of the Koryak tent is very substantial, and capable of withstanding the strongest wind. The thongs which connect the wooden parts make the tent flexible and elastic. During a heavy snow-storm the tent creaks and shakes like a ship at sea; but when the storm is over, it settles back as firm as ever, unless the wind should have broken the lashings.

—WALDEMAR JOCHELSON, *The Koryak*

The frame of the yaranga begins with a tripod of thick poles ten to sixteen feet long. A pole tied across the tripod is used to suspend pots over the central hearth. Around the tripod stakes are set in a circle fifteen to thirty feet in diameter. The stakes, four to five feet in length, are made in sets of two or three and fastened at the top with thongs. Horizontal poles are lashed to the tops of the stakes to form a polygon. At each junction of stake and horizontal pole a roof pole is lashed with its top resting on the tripod. In addition, T poles with curved top pieces are set under the roof poles. Pushing the roof poles upward, they give the roof a curve so that it has a dome shape. This is important so that the snow blows over and off the roof; if it collected on the roof, it might collapse it.

The average-sized tent cover is made of forty reindeer skins from which the fur has been clipped to lighten the tent. The winter tent is made of skins

KORYAK~CHUKCHI YARANGA

Chukchi & Koryak yarangas are essentially the same in construction. The Chukchi tent is smaller, housing 3 or 4 inner tents, the Koryak larger, housing 6 to 8 inner tents.

To set up the frame, first the inner tripod is set up. Next, the wall poles and last the roof poles, the tops resting on the tripod.

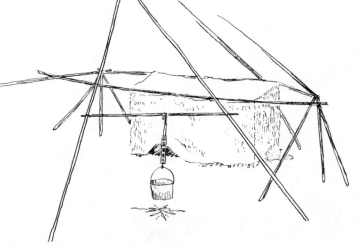

Around the walls are placed the pologs, the inner tents. A horizontal pole tied to the tripod is used to suspend the pot over the fire.

Group of Koryaks outside their communal tent.
Sledges on roof hold cover against the wind.

Men's knife

Women's knife

Skins drying

Working a skin with a scraper.

Antler pot hook

Chukchi tents

Snow beater for beating pologs

previously used for the inner sleeping tents, while the summer tent is made from a worn winter tent. The cover is made in several pieces that are lashed to the frame. A piece of walrus gut is sometimes inserted for a window. The lower ends of the cover are tucked inside and stones are placed on them. In the winter, stakes are lashed to the outside of the cover and water is poured over them —which freezes and holds the tent in place. In stormy weather the Koryak tie their sleds to the roof to hold it down. The Chukchi suspend heavy rocks from the roof edge for the same purpose. In cold weather snow is heaped around the walls to insulate them.

THE INTERIOR

Crawling on hands and knees a distance of twelve or fifteen feet through the low doorway, we entered the large open circle in the interior of the tent. A crackling fire of resinous pine boughs burned brightly upon the ground in the center, illuminating redly the framework of black, glossy poles, and flickering fitfully over the dingy skins of the roof and the swarthy tatooed faces of the women who squatted around. A large copper kettle, filled with some mixture of questionable odour and appearance, hung over the blaze, and furnished occupation to a couple of skinny bare-armed women, who with the same sticks were attentively stirring its contents, poking up the fire, and knocking over the head two or three lazy dogs. The smoke, which rose lazily from the fire, hung in a blue, clearly defined cloud about five feet from the ground, dividing the atmosphere of the tent into a lower stratum of comparatively clean air, and an upper cloud region where smoke, vapours and ill odors contented for supremacy.

—GEORGE KENNAN, *Tent Life in Siberia*

The yaranga is so large because it shelters a very communal people. The Koryak in particular like to live close to one another, and the log houses that shelter the sedentary tribes are built on the same plan. Each family housed in the tent has its own area around the perimeter of the tent, but all share the great fire at the center.

The yaranga shelters a whole set of other tents within it—the *pologs* or sleeping tents. These are tied to the wall poles and house the tent families at night. The central fire of the yaranga is allowed to go out and the cold seeps in through the smoke hole turning the main tent icy cold. The families retreat to the pologs. These are heated with body heat and oil lamps just as the Inuit do in their snow houses. The floor of the polog is made like a large mattress of willow twigs covered with deerskins. The pologs accumulate moisture during the night so that in the morning the Chukchi women take the tents outside;

Large Koryak tent used for a fair

the moisture freezes, turns to ice, and is beaten out, an arduous task. The Koryak only lift up the front corner of the pologs to air them out, a less satisfactory method.

THE CHORAMA DYU

The *chorama dyu* is a sort of refined yaranga. The design of the tent is the same in principle, but the chorama dyu is more systematic and regular in its construction. It is also smaller and lighter, and is used by the tundra divisions of the Even, Evenk, and Yukaghir tribes. The taiga dwellers of these tribes use the conical tent.

The frame begins with a pyramid of four poles of poplar or willow. A horizontal pole is tied across these and holds the cooking pot over the hearth. Around this pyramid are placed the wall sticks in a circle about ten feet in diameter. These sticks are attached to each other with thongs in groups of three; two sticks rest on the ground while the third lies horizontally and is attached to the next group of three . . . and so on around the perimeter. The roof poles rest on the apex of the triangles with their tops resting on the pyramid. The walls stand about four feet high; the top of the tent is around ten feet high.

A close look at this frame construction shows it to be a step closer to the yurt frame than the yaranga. The wall poles do not cross one another as they do in the yurt, but at each junction they are lashed with thongs through holes in the poles. If these holes are moved down and the poles crossed over one another, we have a "folding X"—the basis for yurt folding walls. The roof poles of the chorama dyu also meet at the junction of the wall poles, just as they do in the yurt. Add a tension band to replace the horizontal poles, and we have a true yurt frame.

The cover of the chorama dyu is made of dressed, dehaired reindeer skins. This makes the cover lighter than that used for the yaranga, but not as warm. Three sections of sewn skins are used to cover the roof and two sections to cover the walls. The Evenks sew rectangular pieces of birch bark to the wall cover which makes a strikingly beautiful white tent. Inhabitants of the Okhotsk coast make their tent covers from fishskin. Some seminomads make a semiportable structure by driving wall sticks into the ground, lashing roof poles to these, and covering the whole with larch bark.

CONICAL TENTS

Conical tents are found throughout the entire circumpolar zone with a great variety of frame systems and coverings. The conical tent undoubtedly originated in Siberia and spread west into Lapp country and east into North America. Every group that adopted the conical developed its own unique type and adapted a great variety of materials to this form. That the conical tent spread so far with such wide variety attests to its great antiquity.

The most important element that distinguishes one conical tent from another is the foundation of the frame. The frame poles are not piled on top of one another in a haphazard manner, but are always placed in an established

Evenk birch bark.

Large summer tent of Ancient Yakut.

Orok birch bark

Birch bark door

Soyot summer tents

order. The foundation consists of a set number of poles that are lashed to one another to create a stable framework on which to build the cone. (A house foundation has a similar function.) Once the foundation is built, other poles are set against it to complete the frame. There is an endless variety of foundations: Some are simply three or four straight poles lashed together at the apex; others use specially made poles that are bent and/or have holes in them. The Lapp bent-pole *kata* is the most elaborate of this type of conical tent.

Coverings for the conical tents in Siberia may be of skin, felt, bark, or rush mats depending on the locality and type of people using the tent. Reindeer nomads of the north use only reindeer skin, while nomads of the south use birch bark in their summer tent. Some southern seminomads use rush mats or even felt as yurt dwellers do. The cover is always made by women and the tent is pitched and furnished by them. The men manufacture the wooden parts of the tent as well as other wooden articles such as sleds, skis, and pack saddles.

TAIGA CONICAL TENTS

In areas where trees are plentiful—the *taiga*—the frame of the tent is left standing and only the cover is moved. It is less work to cut a new set of poles than to carry the old ones along. Because of this, these frames are fairly crude and unelaborate when compared to the portable frame of the tundra peoples. A three-pole foundation is used by most taiga peoples with twenty to thirty-five poles of willow or poplar added to complete the frame. The apex of the frame is bound with a bark rope or ring of twisted willow rods.

The summer cover is made of birch bark. In the spring, the bark is stripped from the trees in pieces sixteen to twenty-five feet in length. Each strip is then rolled to form a tube, filled with moss, and steamed for three days to make it pliable. These strips are dried and then sewn together with spruce root into large sections. Four to six sections are used to cover a tent, and are wound around the tent and tied to the frame. Poles are then leaned against this bark cover to keep it in place.

Covers of reindeer skin are used for the winter tent. Skins are soaked in water for a time and left to rot. This loosens the fur and flesh which is then scraped off. These are then tanned with a mixture of water and deer liver. The tanned skins are smoked for several days to make them water repellant and pounded to make them soft. The cover is made in three sections which are wound around the tent, tied down, and held in place by poles leaned against the outside.

TUNDRA CONICAL TENTS

The tents of the Nganasan and the Nentsy of the tundra are built on a foundation of three poles. One of the foundation poles has two or three holes bored into it. A second pole has notches cut in it and is threaded into the first pole so that the notches lodge in the hole. A third pole is placed in the fork of the first two and lashed to it to complete the foundation. Two horizontal poles are lashed across this tripod to suspend cooking pots over the hearth. Thirty to fifty poles are then added to the tripod to complete the cone.

The winter cover for the tent is made of two layers of clipped reindeer skin

BIRCH-BARK CONICAL

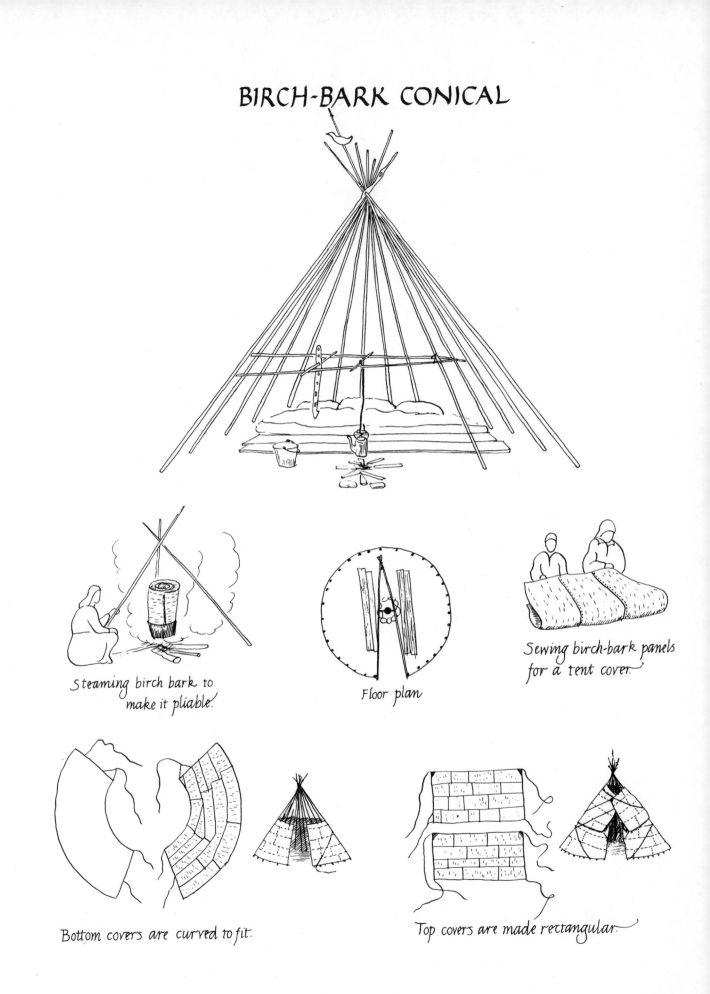

Steaming birch bark to make it pliable.

Floor plan

Sewing birch-bark panels for a tent cover.

Bottom covers are curved to fit.

Top covers are made rectangular.

with the fur facing out. Each cover is made in two parts with pockets sewn into the corners so that the cover may be lifted onto the frame with a couple of poles. Ropes are either sewn to the cover or are attached to a pole and wound around the tent to hold the cover down. The door, which fills the space left where the covers meet, is made so that it can open either right or left depending on wind direction. In the winter the tent is banked with snow to half its height to insulate it and cut out drafts at the tent's edge. A draft hole has to be dug opposite the entrance for the fire to draw properly.

The shaman of each tribe pitches a specially made tent which he surrounds with wooden carvings representing spirit animals. The conical frame incorporates a young birch tree stripped of its lower branches and placed so that its lower end rests on the sacred area (just behind the hearth), while its branched top sits above the smoke hole. This pole is the clan tree that connects the upper (sky), middle (earth), and lower (underground) worlds. It signifies the collective soul of the clan and aids the shaman in his travels through these three worlds.

THE INTERIOR

The interior of the tent is always smoke filled, an advantage in the summer as it keeps the mosquitoes out of the tent. The hearth is a simple circle of stone set in the center of the floor. The floor of the tent is covered with willow twigs with reindeer skins thrown over them. The Evenks simply place sleeping bags around the hearth, but the Yukaghirs set up small sleeping tents for the married couples and single women—the unmarried men, children, and old people sleep on the floor in the cold.

The Nganasan place planks or logs on either side of the hearth demarcating a work area between them and dividing the tent into two rooms, one for the women and one for the men. The area just behind the hearth and against the back wall are designated "clean" or sacred areas where ritual offerings are placed to propitiate the gods of the tribe. During the long winter nights the interior is lighted with tallow lamps or deer-fat candles. The inside of the tent walls are decorated with pieces of birch bark, mica, and pieces of bright cloth. As they move in the draft, they catch the candle light so that the whole inside of the tent appears to be alive, but usually the only light available is from the hearth fire itself. This fire is considered sacred by many Siberian tribes. It is the special property of the tent family—their "spirit"—and outsiders are not allowed to borrow even a light from it.

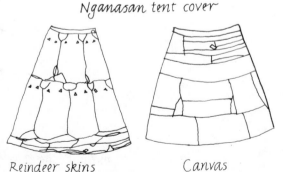

Nganasan tent cover

Reindeer skins   Canvas

Nganasan inner sleeping tents

REINDEER CONICAL

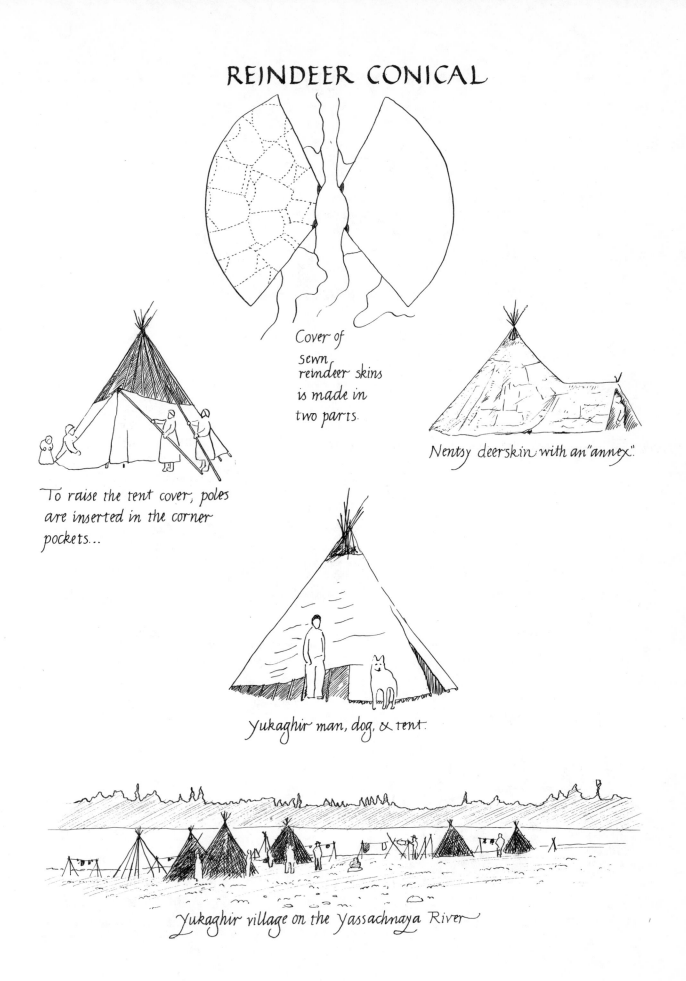

Cover of sewn reindeer skins is made in two parts.

To raise the tent cover, poles are inserted in the corner pockets...

Nentsy deerskin with an "annex".

Yukaghir man, dog, & tent.

Yukaghir village on the Yassachnaya River

BARK DWELLINGS

Nanay dome. Roof of birch bark, walls of rush mats.

Weaving a tent mat

Tuvan four-sided Todzha covered with elm bark.

Khant birch-bark summer tent.

These dwellings
are not truly nomadic,
but the coverings are,
so that sometimes
the cover is moved
while the frame is left.

CHAPTER FIVE

THE LAPP TENT

THE LAPPS

Really the Lapps have almost the same nature as reindeer, both of them migrate north and south and both of them are a little shy.

—JOHAN TURI, *Turi's Book of Lapland*

West of Siberia is Lapland—home of the Lapps. These tough but sensitive people originally migrated from Siberia and have a culture very similar to that of northern Siberians such as the Nentsy and Nganasan. They were originally hunters and fishermen who domesticated reindeer only to move their camps, but influenced by cattle farmers to the south, they began to keep deer for meat and milk. As the last wild deer disappeared they turned to full-time nomadism.

Today only a minority of Lapps are nomadic. These are the mountain or "Fell" Lapps who summer on the mountain tundra and live year round in tents. South of the Fell Lapps dwell the forest Lapps who are seminomads and live in tents only during the summer. On the coasts, sedentary Lapps live in log and turf houses. The number of true nomads is steadily declining; the snowmobile has changed the necessity for frequent changes so that few Lapps are tent dwellers anymore.

The Lapps "herd" reindeer in a very loose sense. The deer follow the same sequence of migration and routes as they would in the wild, and the Lapps can only follow them. But the Lapps benefit the herd in a number of ways. They keep predators—wolves, bears, and wolverines—at bay, especially important at calving time. In the winter the herdsman digs down with his snow shovel and finds moss for the deer, and when the deer can't forage, he cuts down lichen-covered spruce for food. In the summer he builds a smudge fire to keep the mosquitoes and flys away from the deer.

The tools that the Lapp needs to survive the tough Arctic environment have been refined over thousands of years to a perfection and beauty rarely found anywhere in the world. Household goods are few, but every tool and utensil is made of the best materials the Lapps can find and ornamented with a maze of incised designs. Their clothing is beautifully embroidered in bold colors, and one can tell what area a Lapp is from by the design of the clothes.

Two Lapp inventions are essential to life on the move, and without them full nomadism would have never developed in Lapp country—the *akja* and the ski. The akja, the extraordinary Lapp sled, was developed for travel over the light, loose taiga snow. This sled is made in the manner of a fine lap-strake boat with a keel, bent ribs, and lapped planking. There is an akja for every task—open for freight and passengers, closed for carrying food and valuables, and open-ended for carrying tent poles.

The ski is just as essential for winter travel as the akja. The Lapps probably invented the ski, and they are unsurpassed at skiing over the rough terrain of their homeland. Their skis are pointed at both ends and the skier uses a single pole that has a small snow shovel at the top, which he uses to search out winter pasture.

In the spring, before May calving, the reindeer move to the foothills of the mountains. The akjas are loaded and each is hitched to a draft reindeer which is tied to the akja in front . . . and so on down the line making a long train. The trip must be made at night when the snow is frozen. The spring camp lasts for a month; they then move to their mountain pastures. Camp is struck: The tent cloth goes on the back of a deer as padding and the poles are lashed to either side. Goods are packed in oval chests and tied to either side of a pack saddle. A gentle deer with a cradle and infant on its back leads off and the caravan ascends the mountains.

In the autumn the deer move down from the mountains. They are rounded up and corraled and sorting takes place. The Lapps are expert with the lasso, and snare the deer by the antlers. Every deer owner knows his animals by the notches he cuts in the ears. Culled deer are slaughtered and their meat dried for the lean times ahead. The akjas are again loaded as the herd heads to the forest for the winter. The long winter night descends, and the Lapps stay inside and work at making and repairing their possessions.

LAPP TRAVEL

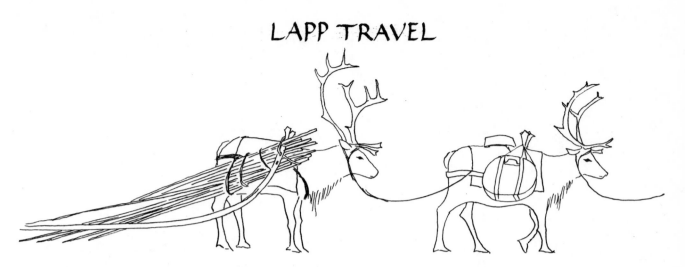

The last reindeer in the train carries the tent poles. The others carry the tent cover & chests containing food, utensils & tools.

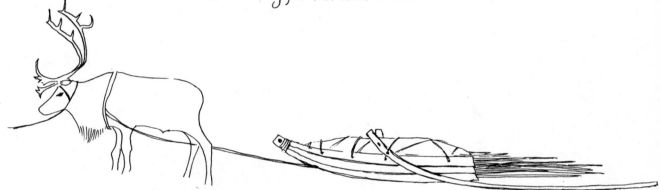

The last akja in the train has the back open so that it can carry the tent poles.

The Lapps travel on skis in winter. Lapp shoes have turned up toes so that they hold the skis from slipping off the foot. The binding is a simple leather loop.

A Lapp herdsman always carries a lasso over his shoulder & a knife on his belt. His single ski pole has a small snow shovel at one end so that he can dig for moss beneath the snow for the reindeer herds.

LAPP SPRING CAMP

THE KATA

There is nothing primitive about the Lapp tent. Let us take into full consideration the requirements that such a moveable tent should fulfill. It should be easily transportable; no single part should be too heavy or too cumbersome to constitute one half of the burden of the pack reindeer (maximum weight 40 lbs.). In case any part is lost or damaged during migration, it should be possible to replace or repair it. It should be big enough for a numerous family to eat and sleep and entertain guests in. I do not know whether the military experts of the western world have managed to meet these requirements better than the Scandinavian Lapps have done.

—BJORN COLLINDER, *The Lapps*

Kata is the Lapp name for their conical homes. There are three types: turf kata, forked-pole kata, and curved-pole kata. The turf kata is a sedentary house. It uses the same basic frame system as the curved-pole kata, but the frame is much heavier and the structure is covered with logs and turf. The forked-pole kata is built much like other semiportable tents of the taiga. The frame, which is a cone of forked poles, is left standing when the Lapps move and only the cover is moved. The curved-pole kata is the true nomad tent and the only one used by nomads year round.

The curved-pole kata is a unique Lapp invention. No other conical tent uses such a foundation of curved rafters. This frame allows for a larger diameter conical tent to be made without using longer poles. Other conical tents have to increase pole length as the tent diameter increases—which means a heavier frame. (The Plains Indians could only increase the diameter of the tipi when they obtained the horse to carry the longer tent poles.) There is one disadvantage to the kata—the smoke hole is quite large, and in the winter snow sometimes fills the tent and must be shoveled out. But the Lapps say that the smoke hole has to be large because they build big fires, and the fire usually takes care of any rain or snow that comes in the tent.

The curved poles of the kata frame are made from two pairs of naturally bow-shaped pines or birches. The sides are squared off and holes are bored near the end and in the middle. Each pair of rafters is threaded onto the end of the "smoke pole" at the top and onto a cross piece in the middle. In addition, two doorposts, shaped like hockey sticks, are threaded onto the smoke pole in the front. A single pole in the rear completes the foundation. There are two holes in the top of each rafter and doorpost so that the tent can be made a little bit larger or smaller.

This framework of ten poles is quite strong and can easily support a person standing on it. Against this frame are laid twelve to eighteen slender poles from nine to fifteen feet long. A few of these are held by loops on the frame, and in rough weather, all the poles may be lashed down with rope.

The tent cover is made in two halves which are fastened together at the single back pole. The free ends of the cover are pulled around the tent and lashed to the door poles. In the past, the summer cover was birch bark sewn

TURF KATA

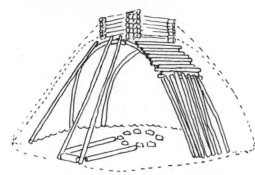

The turf kata uses the same frame system as the curved-pole kata. This is the home of the forest Lapps in the winter & the coastal Lapps year round.

Turf kata with goats.

FORKED-POLE KATA

A three-pole foundation of forked poles...

...with 20 to 30 poles added.

The forked-pole kata is used by seminomadic Forest Lapps in the summer. The frame is left standing & only the cover is moved.

CURVED-POLE KATA

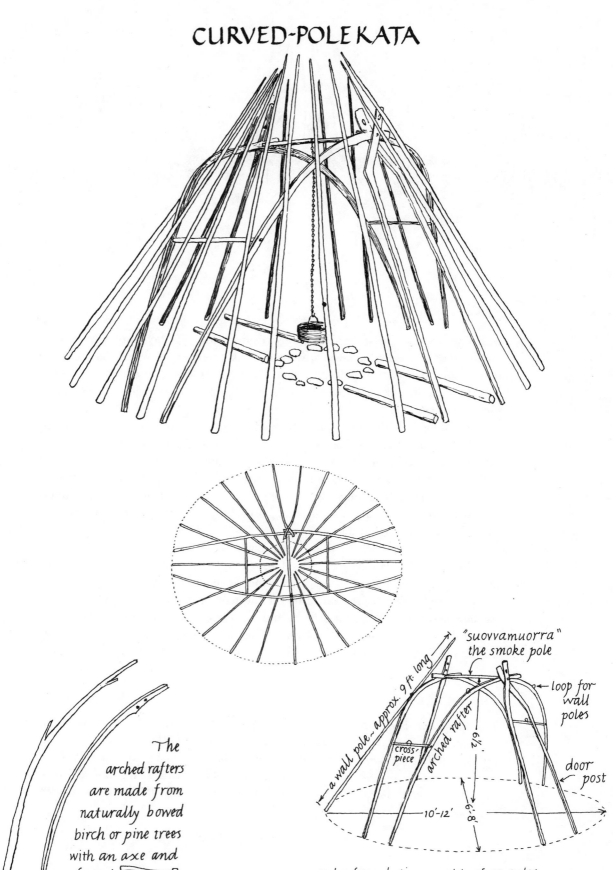

The arched rafters are made from naturally bowed birch or pine trees with an axe and a knife!

"suovvamuorra" the smoke pole

a wall pole ~ approx. 9 ft. long

cross-piece

arched rafter

loop for wall poles

door post

9'

8'-9"

10'-12'

The foundation consists of 10 poles.

Pitching Lapp tents

with sinew, while the winter cover was reindeer skins. Today canvas is used in the summer and a double layer of woolen blankets covers the winter tent. Sometimes a square of linen is placed on the back side of the tent to admit light. The tent cloth is pulled up and fastened with the help of a ladder made from a naturally forked tree.

The door is made of cloth or skins and has wooden battens fastened to it to hold it flat against the doorposts. The threshold is made of a board fastened to the doorposts with thongs. Anchor stones are sometimes used on the edge of the cloth to hold it down. These leave evidence of past campsites and are found all over Lapland. In stormy weather the akjas are leaned against the tent to hold the cover down, but even so some storms blow the tent cover away leaving the occupants huddled in the cold.

The tents are pitched in sheltered places close to wood and water. The country is usually familiar and the Lapps favor old campsites that have the hearth stones and anchor stones of previous tents already in place. When the camp is reached everyone hurries to get the tent up before dark: The women cut boughs, arrange them for a floor, and put the tent up over them; the chests and bedding are brought in and placed against the walls; a fire is lit in the hearth and within an hour everyone is settled in their cozy tent.

THE INTERIOR

The Lapp tent is a little cosmos. All the different utensils and other household goods are put in their place after they have been used; nothing is lost or spoiled by neglect. The tasks and occupations of the different members of the household are regulated by ancient usage, and so are the places which they and different categories of guests occupy when sitting down or lying near the boasso or nearer the door.

—BJORN COLLINDER, *The Lapps*

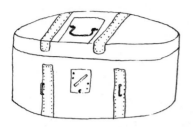

The bent-wood chest is the only furniture found in a Lapp tent. One or two chests hold all the tools & utensils a Lapp family needs. The chests are lashed to either side of a pack saddle or placed in an akja when the Lapps travel.

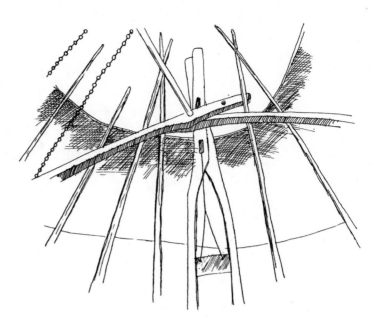

Looking upward & forward where the smoke pole joins the arched rafters and the door-posts

The floor of the kata is covered with twigs. Furs or blankets over these make beds. Chains with hooks suspend pots over the hearth.

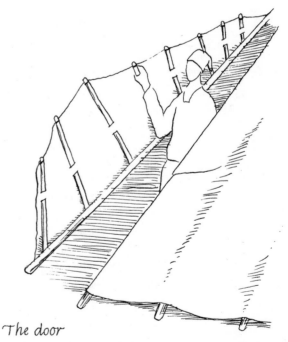

The door is like a sail with battens. Suspended from the top & attached to one side it swings open like a hinged door.

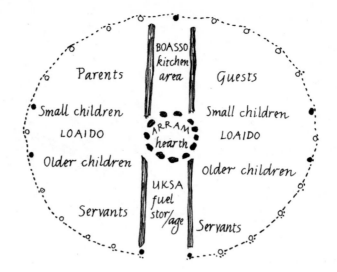

At the center of the tent is the hearth—a ring of flat stones. Over it a chain with a hook on the end dangles down from the smoke pole to suspend kettles and to smoke reindeer meat. The tent floor is divided into rooms. Two parallel logs run from the doorposts to the hearth and contain the *uksa* where firewood is stored. On the opposite side of the hearth two more parallel logs enclose the *boasso,* the kitchen area where food is prepared. This is also a sacred area where the shaman's drum is kept. The Lapps believe that when a person dies the body must be taken out the boasso side of the tent or another person will die in the tent.

The hearth, the uksa, and the boasso divide the kata into two rooms. These are the living and sleeping space—the *loaido.* The floor of this space is covered with a thick layer of spruce boughs or birch twigs and covered with reindeer skins. Rolled up coats placed against the walls make cushions. Sleeping bags are made of reindeer fur or sheepskin with a pocket at the end for the feet. Northern Lapps hang a mosquito net over each bed. Some Lapps use a linen sleeping tent suspended from the tent poles for warmth in the winter.

A fire is kept going in the hearth day and night. Smoke fills the interior to within a few feet of the floor. This keeps the mosquitoes out, but in bad weather the smoke may completely fill the tent blinding everyone. In extremely cold weather—forty below—a huge fire is kept going and the flames reach almost to the smoke pole. Much of the heat goes up with the flames, so as one is roasted in front, he freezes in back. Condensation from breath and cooking creates an ice fog which hangs in the tent so that the tent dwellers can barely see from one side to the other, but the Lapps are a hardy people and wouldn't have it any other way—the kata is their home.

CHAPTER SIX

THE INUIT TENT

THE INUIT

Eskimos understood the true art of living. They did not simply exist. Men, women and children took a tremendous and vital joy from the hour-by-hour activities of their lives. They exercised an almost unparalleled genius at inventing and constructing useful equipment without the benefit of engineering science or mechanical technology.

— FARLEY MOWAT, *Canada North*

The Inuit were traditionally nomads. They moved their hunting and fishing camps with the same regularity with which pastoral nomads moved their herding camps. Each animal that provided food to the Inuit had a particular time and place in which it could be hunted, and the Inuit moved accordingly. The Inuit depended on animals even more than the pastoralist, for most Inuit diets contained no plant food.

Inuit migrations were irregular, reflecting the irregularity of the animal migrations. In the winter, camps were made offshore on the sea ice for seal hunting. The men spread out to hunt the seal at their breathing holes; the women hooked tom cod through holes chopped in the ice. But by midwinter it was dark day and night and little hunting or fishing could be done. This was the time for the repair and manufacture of equipment and clothes and for story telling. The men recited the tribal tales of how the world was made and where the animal people came from. A great snowhouse was built for a festival of singing, dancing, and feasting.

Spring was an ambivalent season. Light and warmth returned, but the game became scarce—starvation was all too frequent. Winter camps broke up and families camped on the river banks to spear fish and await the caribou at their crossings. For the inland peoples who could not move by kayak or umiak, this time was particularly difficult as everything had to be carried on one's back through the marshy tundra. But as summer arrived, game and fish became plentiful again, and the siege of starvation and want was over.

Fall was the season of abundance. The fish were fat, the mosquitoes were gone, and caribou fur for clothing was at its best. Arctic char were speared and dried for the lean times ahead. Caribou were hunted as they migrated south, and their meat dried and cached.

Throughout these travels over the treeless tundra, one article was critical to Inuit survival—the soapstone lamp. Burning seal or whale oil, it gives a steady, if low, flame which provides heat and light. Food was cooked over this lamp in soapstone kettles, and wet clothing was dried on a rack above it. Because of the lamp, work could continue during the long winter darkness, and Inuit dwellings could be made without a smoke hole so that no heat escaped—all other arctic peoples had to use tents with smoke holes. The combination of body heat and warmth from the lamp kept the Inuit dwellings—whether snowhouse, turfhouse, or tent—remarkably warm.

THE INUIT TENT

The familiar Western notion of enclosed space is foreign to the Aivilik. Both winter igloos and summer sealskin tents are dome-shaped. Both lack vertical walls and horizontal ceilings; no planes parallel each other and none intersect at 90 degrees. There are no straight lines, at least none of any length.

Visually and acoustically the igloo is "open," a labyrinth alive with the movements of crowded people. No flat static walls arrest the ear or eye, but voices and laughter come from several directions and the eye can glance through here, past there, catching glimpses of the activities of nearly everyone. The same is true of the sealskin tent. Every sound outside can be heard within, and the women inside always seem to be turning and stretching so they can peer out through holes in the tent.

—EDMUND CARPENTER, *Eskimo*

MOVING

TENT BECOMES SLEDGE   In the fall the tent skins are sometimes used to make a sledge. The skins are dipped in water in a hole in the ice & wrapped around frozen fish.

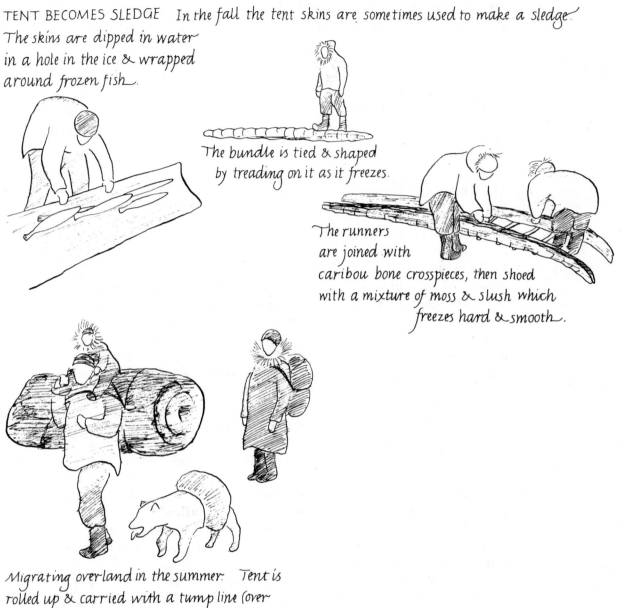

The bundle is tied & shaped by treading on it as it freezes.

The runners are joined with caribou bone crosspieces, then shoed with a mixture of moss & slush which freezes hard & smooth.

Migrating overland in the summer. Tent is rolled up & carried with a tump line (over forehead) & breast line. Eskimo men have been known to carry over 400 pounds in this way. Dogs can carry 30 to 40 pounds.

The umiak is the usual way of moving for coastal Eskimos.

No nomadic people possess such a variety of tents as the Inuit, and no people have ever devised tents with such a minimal use of solid material—one Inuit tent uses only a single pole. They are also the only people to make tents exclusively from animal matter—one Inuit tent is made from only the skin and bones of walrus and seal.

There are three basic types of Inuit tent—the ridge, the conical, and the dome. The type is determined by the frame—which is controlled by the number of poles that can be obtained. The ridge tent is used where wood is scarce in northern Alaska, Canada, and in Greenland. The conical and dome tents require more poles and are used by Inuit closer to the forests of Alaska and Canada.

RIDGE TENT

The ridge tent exists in a great variety of forms which attests to its great antiquity. It is predominate in Greenland, Labrador, and Baffin Island, but is found as far west as Point Barrow, Alaska. The ridge tent is the most characteristically Inuit tent. The dome and the conical tent can be traced to contact with the Indians just to the south of Inuit country, but the ridge tent is uniquely Inuit.

The single feature common to all ridge tents is the ridgepole supported by one or more upright poles. In wood-scarce regions only a single upright pole with a short ridgepiece may be used. If there is no wood to be had, the center pole is made of spliced antler or bone (the penis bone of the walrus is sometimes used). The Inuit possess marvelous skill at piecing together short sections to make long members for sled runners, boat frames, and harpoons. The spliced pieces often possess greater strength than a single piece of wood.

The typical ridge tent of the Central Inuit is made with ten poles. The foundation is made of two pairs of crossed poles set at a distance from each other and connected by a double ridgepole. Four more poles are set against the rear poles to make a half cone. The rear of the tent thus becomes a little wider and higher, and this is where the occupants sit. Where less wood is to be had, various parts of this frame are eliminated. The half cone in the rear is often left off, and the ridgepoles may be replaced with a line strung between the crossed poles. The variations are endless, but in general an attempt is made to give the tent the typical wedge shape.

The Greenland Inuit build a different variety of ridge tent. They use a very long ridgepole, resting it on the ground in the rear of the tent and supporting it high up—six to ten feet—at the front with two poles supporting a short piece. The frame may be just these four poles but the Greenlanders often add additional pieces to the frame to gain more space inside. The sealskin cover is made with holes down the front so that it can be lashed together like a shoe.

The tent covering is made of untanned skins. Fat and flesh are scraped off the skins and they are stretched to dry. Hair is left on the skins except for those used next to the entrance which are cut thin and transparent to let in light. The preferred skin comes from the largest square flipper seal since it is too heavy for other uses. Caribou skin is warmer than seal (the hairs are hollow and insulate), but it is not as durable. Any fur skin is used in a pinch, even walrus and musk ox. The number of skins used varies with the size of the tent, ten to fifteen

RIDGE

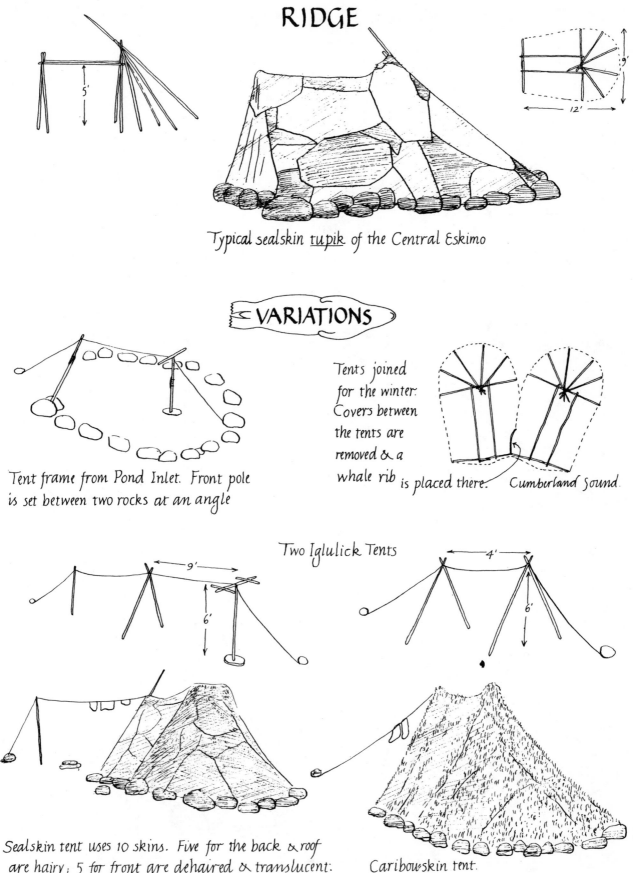

Typical sealskin <u>tupik</u> of the Central Eskimo

VARIATIONS

Tent frame from Pond Inlet. Front pole is set between two rocks at an angle

Tents joined for the winter. Covers between the tents are removed & a whale rib is placed there.   Cumberland Sound.

Two Iglulick Tents

Sealskin tent uses 10 skins. Five for the back & roof are hairy; 5 for front are dehaired & translucent.

Caribouskin tent.

GREENLAND

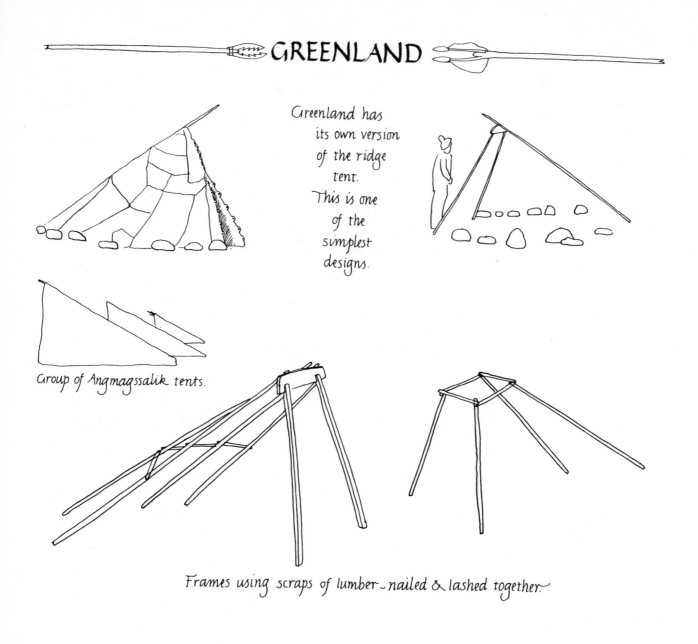

Greenland has its own version of the ridge tent. This is one of the simplest designs.

Group of Angmagssalik tents.

Frames using scraps of lumber - nailed & lashed together.

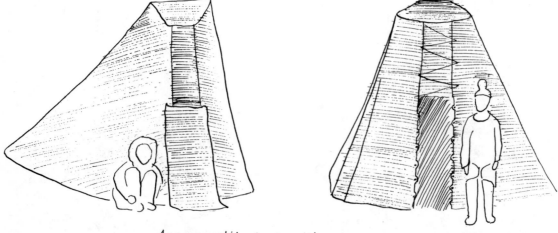

Angmagssalik tents with canvas covers.

seal skins being average. Tent skins are sewn together by the women using sinew from caribou or white whale, an ivory needle, and a sealskin thimble. The guy lines holding the tent are made of plaited sinew which is very strong.

Though almost none of the traditional Inuit tents are being used today, the ridge tent survives in a somewhat altered form. The white canvas wall tent adopted from the white man is used everywhere in the summer. In size and shape it is close to the traditional tent, and contemporary Inuit sew them together from commercial canvas or buy them ready made.

CONICAL TENT

The Inuit conical tent was probably adopted from the Indian conical tent found to the south. It is quite similar to the Cree tent, but does not have a smoke hole such as Indian tents do. The conical tent is favored by the Caribou Inuit and by some Alaskan and Central Canadian Inuits.

The tent uses a two pole foundation. Two poles eleven to fifteen feet long are tied at the top with a babiche (rawhide) or sealskin line which is used to hold the two poles leaning at an angle while two more poles are laid in the fork. Another three or four poles are put up, and the line is wound around the cone to strengthen it. Sometimes sled runners are used for poles. One version of the conical tent used at Point Barrow, Alaska, has only four or five poles twelve feet in length. Halfway up these poles a hoop of willow rods is lashed, and shorter poles—spears, umiak oars, etc.—are laid on the hoop.

The cover for the conical tent is usually caribou, although some coastal peoples use seal. Ten to twenty deerskins are sewn in a half circle. A row of dehaired translucent skins along the front edge let in light. The tent sheet is drawn over the back of the tent and around to either side of the doorway where it is lashed. Western Alaskan tribes make the cover in two pieces which are wound around the frame in a spiral. Stones are rolled onto the edge of the cover on the outside to hold it in place.

CONICAL

SETTING UP THE TENT

①

The two front poles are tied at their tops with a long line & held leaning back.

②

Two other poles are laid in the fork of the first two.

③

Three or four other poles are put up. The line is then wound several times around to strengthen the frame.

④

The skin cover is drawn over the frame from back to front & laced together over the door.

On the Western Alaska coast there is a variant of the conical. Four or five long poles make the cone. Halfway up a hoop is lashed around the circumference. Shorter poles, umiak oars, spears, etc. are leaned against the hoop.

The cover is usually made in a semicircle.

Padlimiut conical of caribou skin at Eskimo Point, Hudson Bay.

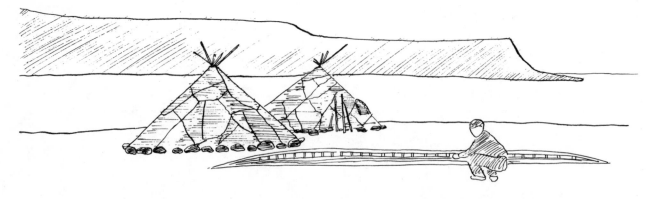

Making a kayak ~ Little Whale River, Hudson Bay.

THE DOME TENT

It is a good warm home in bitter cold. The tent rides out the storms like a snow hut, and is also convenient to transport on a sledge, even if it is rather heavy when the frost has bitten deep into the skins. It is a firm, solid object in the landscape, like a dome-shaped granite rock.

—HELGE INSTAD, *Nunamiut*

The dome is thought to be the original Inuit dwelling. At one time widespread, it is now used only by inland tribes of North Alaska and the Mackenzie River area. The dome must have been the predecessor of the snowhouse: Domes are always covered with snow, and if the tent is removed after the snow hardens, a free-standing snow dome is left. At some time in the past an inventive Inuit learned to construct the snow dome without using the tent.

The frame of the dome tent is made of two dozen willow rods twelve to fifteen feet in length. These are driven into the ground in a rough circle. Opposing poles are bent toward each other and tied together. A number of caribou skins sewn together with the fur side out are thrown over the frame. Another layer of dehaired skins or canvas is placed over this and is held in place with rocks or pegs tied to it. At the doorway, a high threshold of turf is built up to keep out drafts. A bearskin is used for the door. A sheet of bear intestine is sometimes used for a window—nowadays glass is used.

A typical Nunamiut dome is about nine by ten feet and about five and a half feet high at the center. Up to twenty people can be seated inside, but for a festival the wall poles are moved out and as many as sixty can squeeze in. The floor is covered with willow twigs and in the back third of the tent a bed of caribou skins is made. Bundles of skins, storage sacks, and sleeping bags line the walls. In modern times, a stove, located just to the right of the entrance is used for heat.

The dome is the only tent used by the Inuit in the winter. Some still use this tent to create a snowhouse: The willow frame is covered with snow, and heated rocks are brought inside causing the walls to melt; the rocks are removed, the walls freeze, and the frame is removed leaving a snow dome. Occasionally the Nunamiut make rectangular snowhouses and roof them with caribou skins.

Fall arrives. Cold blows through the tent seams. As soon as enough snow falls the men make a snowhouse or the family moves to a turf house, and the tent is put away for the winter. This presents a problem for the cover must be stored on stone posts to keep rodents from eating the skins, and by spring the tent family may be so far away from where they left the tent that they can't return to it. The Netsilik solve this problem by turning their tent into a sled: They douse the tent skins with water, roll them around some frozen fish, and shape this mass into sled runners, which they fasten together with short pieces of wood. In the summer caribou skins—which float—are used to ford rivers. Sometimes the conical tent is used in winter: The tent is covered with shrubs and a second cover is thrown over this. Snow vaults are built over the entrance to keep the wind out.

DOME

Snow is cleared from an area or packed down. Twenty to 30 willow poles, 12 to 15 feet long are planted in the ground in a circle. Opposing poles are bent over & tied to each other.

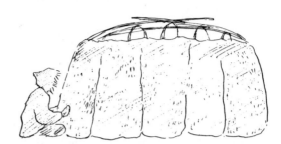

Caribou skins, fur side out, are sewed together to make the inside covering.

Typical dimensions

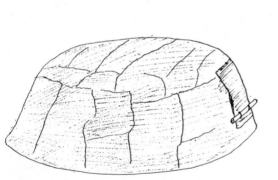

The outside cover is made of dehaired caribou skins sewed together & tied down. The door is kept from blowing open by a log weight.

Contemporary dome. Door is of grizzly bear fur. Canvas covers caribou fur underneath. Glass window replaces traditional one of bear intestine.

Nunamiut camp - Anaktuvuk Pass, Alaska. Tent is canvas covered. Skins dry on rack at center.

Caribou Eskimo Conical

caribou skin bed

fire place

ULU
or women's knife
used in skinning
game, cutting up
meat & cutting
skins. Traditionally
slate, now made of
old saw blades &
bone or antler.

furs & bags

caribou skin bed

tool box

floor of willow twigs

sheet iron stove

Nunamiut Dome

TRADITIONAL ~ Soapstone kettle heated by
soapstone lamp with drying rack above

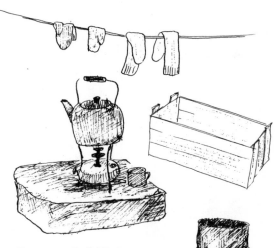

CONTEMPORARY ~
Primus stove heats tea kettle.
Mittens & socks dry above.

Wooden dish

Bone scraper for skins

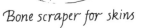

Sealskin cup

CHAPTER SEVEN

TENTS OF THE NORTH AMERICAN TAIGA

INDIAN TRIBES OF THE TAIGA

The North American subarctic region is quite similar to the Siberian taiga. The great spruce forests, the mosquito-infested summers, the long cold winters, the animal life—all are common to both. And the tribes that dwell there follow similar lives: Both use birch-bark canoes, both dwell in bark-and-skin-covered conical and dome tents, and both depend on the same animal—the reindeer of Siberia and the caribou of America. But while the Siberians domesticated their deer, which gave them control over their movements and power for their sleds, the Americans were at the mercy of the caribou's unpredictable migration routes. The Americans' only domesticated animal was the dog, and some tribes had so few dogs that they had to pull their sleds by hand.

TRIBES OF THE SUBARCTIC TAIGA

For the northern Indian tribes the caribou provided all: skins for clothes, tent covers, and sleeping bags; sinews for thread; untanned skin for strips (babiche) for lashings and for snowshoe webbing. Although caribou was the mainstay of the diet, the Indians also ate other game—moose, bear, elk, rabbits, ducks, and geese. Fish, too, were important, especially as dog food—summer camps were always made on the river banks at good fishing spots. But with the exception of the great caribou herds, game was scarce over this area and famine was a common occurrence. Survival was possible only through great hunting skill and the ability to move quickly over great distances. Without the snowshoe, the birch-bark canoe, and the toboggan—all of which were invented by these people—life could not have been possible in this country.

TENTS OF THE NORTH AMERICAN TAIGA

". . . hast thou as much ingenuity and cleverness as the Indians, who carry their houses and their wigwams with them so that they may lodge wheresoever they please, independently of any seigneur whatsoever? Thou art not so bold nor as stout as we, because when thou goest on a voyage thou canst not carry upon thy shoulders thy buildings and thy edifices. Therefore it is necessary that thou preparest as many lodgings as thou makest changes of residence, or else thou lodgest in a hired house which does not belong to thee . . ."

—An Indian chief from Quebec in:
LECLERQ, *Nouvelle Relation de la Gaspesie* (1691)

Two types of semiportable dwelling were once used over almost all the North American taiga—the dome and the conical tent. For both of these tents the frame was left in place and only the cover was moved. Both are generally called "wigwam," (an Algonquian word meaning "dwelling"), but since the term does not distinguish between the conical and the dome it is somewhat misleading. Most tribes used both types at the same time, but the more northern tribes favored the conical exclusively. Each type has its advantages: the dome is superior in the winter since there is less space to heat, but is poor in rainy weather because the roof is prone to leak.

There was also one truly portable tent found in this area: the Kutchin tent, used above the tree line so that both the frame as well as the cover was moved. This tent was halfway between the dome and the cone in shape and had its own unique method of construction.

Cree toboggan

Ojibway birch-bark conical & dome.

THE DOME TENT

The dome tent was found throughout the forested regions of the East from the Atlantic Ocean to the eastern edge of the prairies. A typical example of this tent was the Ojibway "waginogan," which was covered with rush mats, bark, and/or skins; rush mats were commonly used for the walls and birch bark for the roof (an identical type was used in Siberia). Birch bark was always preferred where it was obtainable; when not, elm, black ash, pine, chestnut, or cedar were used. These barks did not have the flexibility of birch bark and had to be heated in a fire to bend them to fit. Mats were made of cattail, bulrush, or grass.

The frame was made of just about any supple wood—willow, hickory, birch, or oak. The Ojibway preferred ironwood since it was pliable but tough when dry so that poles could be made an inch or less in diameter. The poles were stuck in the ground in an oval, slanting slightly outward. Opposing poles were bent toward each other, overlapped a foot or two, and lashed with the inner bark of the basswood. Horizontal poles were then lashed around these to strengthen the frame, and birch bark was placed on the dome in rolls (other bark was put on in slabs). The cover was then tied down with lines attached to pegs set in the ground around the perimeter. A smoke hole was left in the middle of the roof. Some peoples set a piece of mat or bark up as a screen on the windward side of the smoke hole to draw the smoke out—like the smoke flaps of the tipi.

THE CONICAL TENT

These tents are made of Drest Deer skins, or Drest moose skins, which is commonly ten skins, in tent, a moderate tent, will hold twelve or fourteen Indians old and young, they are very cold living on the winter, and subject very much to smoking w'ch the Native does not much mind, sitting on the ground, wherefore the smoak ascending does not Effect their Eyes much, tho Very troublesome to the English men, they not being us'd to such low seats . . .

—JAMES ISHAM, *Observations on Hudson's Bay*
(1743, among the Cree Indians)

OJIBWAY DOMES

① Poles are set in 2 rows, opposing poles are bent over and tied to form an arch.

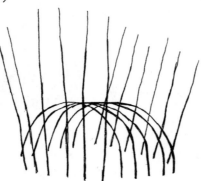

② Poles are set at each end and bent over.

Black ash with birch-bark roof.

Rush mats with birch-bark roof.

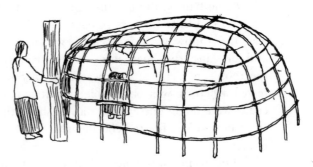

③ Horizontal poles are lashed around the circumference & the bark cover is put on.

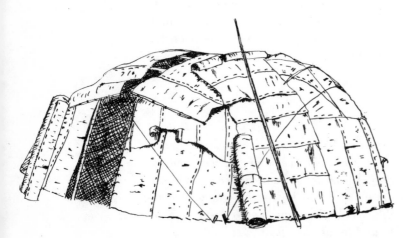

Birch bark is put on in rolls made of a number of sheets sewn together with split spruce roots. The rolls are held down with lines and poles leaned against the wall.

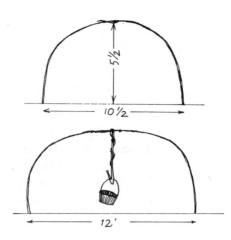

Kickapoo dome

The dominant house type over most of the North American taiga was the simple conical tent. This tent was small and squat when compared to a conical tent such as the tipi. Headroom existed only at the very center (the space occupied by the hearth) but since the tent was smoke filled most of the time, one couldn't stand up anyway. As long as poles were plentiful, the frame was not moved, and there was little pattern to how the frame was set up. The four-pole foundation was the most widespread.

The birch-bark conical was used by a number of northeastern tribes including the Naskapi, Montagnais, Micmac, Abnaki, Penobscot, Ojibway, and Cree. The best information we have on its construction comes from an account of the Penobscot conical by Frank Speck, which I follow here.

The frame was made of twelve-foot-long cedar poles with a foundation made of two pairs of poles tied at the top with cedar bark. Five other poles were laid between these. A hoop of bent willow rods was lashed around the inside about two-thirds up from the bottom. This strengthened the frame and held up a series of horizontal poles which were placed across it and which served as drying racks and to suspend pots over the hearth. Rolls of birch bark were then laid over the frame in three tiers overlapping each other. Nine poles were laid over the bark, each one set opposite an inside pole with the butt end sunk in the ground and the top end lashed to an inside pole across the bark. The bark was thus clamped between the two poles. The door was made of moose hide hung from a pole.

The northern tribes covered their tents with caribou skins. In the winter, winter-killed skins—on which the fur is thick—were used with the hair turned in, while in the summer, dehaired skins were used. South of caribou country, moose, deer, or elk skins were used—sometimes together with birch bark. Often skins were not sewn together but thrown randomly over the frame and held down with poles and lines. Further south, the Ojibway conical tents used birch bark and rush mats. The Thompson and Kutenai of the Pacific Northwest used just mats on their tents since they had no birch bark.

Naskapi

Mixed types: Two birch-bark conicals, a rush mat conical in the foreground & a tipi on the right. Cree tents in Manitoba

Montagnais

Chipewyan caribou skin tent with hinged door and stove pipe buried in the snow.

Ojibway birchbark

PENOBSCOT BIRCH-BARK CONICAL

4-pole foundation

7' 10' 6'

15'

hearth

Ojibwa camp on Lake Huron: Birch-bark & rush-mat conicals ~ after painting by Paul Kane c.1845

Thompson River rush-mat conical tent.

The floor of these tents was covered with a carefully laid bed of spruce boughs over which were placed mats and furs. The hearth was bounded by logs to keep the boughs and bedding out of the fire. In the winter, the Penobscot heated stones on a large fire built outside the tent and carried them inside to keep the interior warm for the night.

North American Interiors

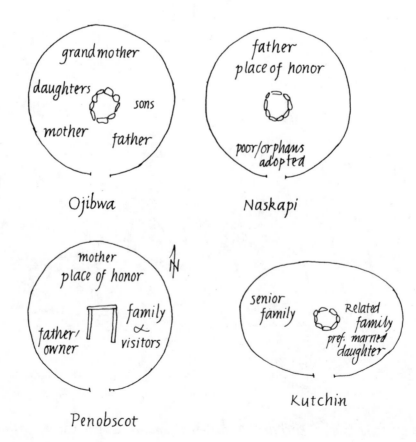

THE KUTCHIN TENT

The Kutchin tent is the only completely portable tent found in the North American taiga. From the outside it looks similar to the dome tent used by the Indians and Inuit of the area, but it is actually very unlike these domes in its construction. The Kutchin tent employs a unique system of arched poles to create a large oval-shaped interior space. Robert McKennan, an ethnologist who spent time with the Kutchin, believes that this tent evolved from the double lean-to (two simple log lean-tos set up facing each other with a fire built between them) which is much used in this area.

The Kutchin tent is used by the Kutchin, Han, and Tanana Indians who live in inland Alaska and the Mackenzie River area. Because these people live close to the tree line they developed a nomadic dwelling for use in areas where poles were unavailable. Tappan Adney—an artist who wrote the definitive account of birch-bark canoe construction—lived with the Han and left an excellent eyewitness description of how this tent is constructed and how it is pitched:

> The women took long-handled wooden shovels and removed the snow off the ground in an elliptical space eighteen feet long by twelve feet wide, banking it all around two feet high. While some covered the exposed river gravel with green spruce boughs and kindled a fire in the center, others cut sticks three to five feet long and set them upright a foot apart in the bank of snow, the long way of the intended house, leaving an opening at one side two feet wide for the door. The house poles, an inch thick and ten or twelve feet long, whittled out of spruce and previously bent and seasoned into the form of a curve, were then set up in the snow at the ends of the camp to the number of sixteen or twenty, their upper ends pointing toward the middle in the form of a dome ten feet high. These were strengthened by two arched cross-poles underneath, the ends of which were lashed to the sidestakes with withes of willow twigs thawed out and made pliant over the fire. Over this comparatively stiff framework next was drawn a covering of caribou skin, tanned with the hair on, made in two sections, and shaped and sewed together to fit the dome. The two sections, comprising forty skins completely covered the house, except in the middle, where a large hole was left for the smoke to escape and at the doorway, over which was hung a piece of blanket.
>
> (ADNEY, *Klondike Stampede*)

Spruce forests were preferred as camping spots so as to gain shelter from the wind and snow. The tents were pitched with the doorway facing south. Often two related families used the same tent, one at each end of the ellipse. This accounts for the fairly large size of this tent when it is compared to other tents of the taiga region. The lodge is designed to be partially snow covered, with only the top third exposed so that it was well insulated. It was reported to look like an upside down tea cup issuing smoke from a hole in its bottom. The tent was the property of women who had the job of moving it along with all the other baggage on toboggans. This left the men free to hunt as the tribe moved about in search of game.

Today, most of the tents described here have disappeared from the taiga, although the Mistassini Cree still use a canvas-covered conical tent in their hunting camps. Most Indian peoples have adopted the ridge-wall tent for their

KUTCHIN TENT

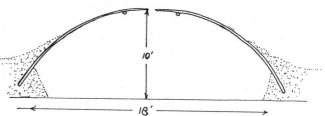

The frame is made of 20 curved poles supported by 2 arches. Additional short poles are set in the front & back.

The Kutchin tent utilizes the taiga snow to hold the poles & as insulation as it covers the roof.

Pots are suspended from the rafters.

After an Adney drawing.

hunting and fishing camps. This design, modeled after the military tent, makes full use of commercial canvas widths with little waste of material and minimal seams—Indian women can sew one together in a day with a hand-cranked sewing machine. They are always left their natural white color and waterproofed with paraffin and turpentine. The rectangular floor plan is well suited to tent platforms with board floors used in more permanent camps.

CHAPTER EIGHT

THE TIPI

AMERICAN PLAINS NOMADS

You ask me to plow the ground! Shall I take a knife and tear my mother's bosom? Then when I die she will not take me to her bosom to rest. You ask me to dig for stone! Shall I dig under her skin for her bones? Then when I die I cannot enter her body to be born again. You ask me to cut the grass and make hay and sell it, and be rich like white men! But how dare I cut off my mother's hair?

—SMOHALLA

Before the introduction of the horse, the North American Plains were home to a few seminomadic tribes who lived most of the year in large communal earth lodges and tilled fields of corn, beans, and squash. They left these homes in the summer and again in the fall to hunt the buffalo, during which time they lived in conical skin tents—tipis. Buffalo meat was an important part of their diet, but corn and beans were as important. The arrival of the horse changed all this.

The horse gave the Plains tribes the mobility to follow the buffalo anywhere and to kill enough to live year round on buffalo meat. The Plains tribes abandoned their earth houses, crops, and settled life and became full-time nomads. Tribes to the east, feeling the pressure of the white advance, moved to the plains and adopted the new way. In a short time the Plains became the home of a vast number of tipi-dwelling nomad tribes.

Except for some roots and berries, buffalo meat became the only food the Plains people consumed. A single man on horseback could kill three or four buffalo in a day, enough to feed his family for a month. Every part of the buffalo was used: the skins for tents, robes, clothing, storage containers, and riding gear; the sinew for thread and bowstrings; bone and horn for tools and utensils; the brains to tan the hides; and the dung for fuel. Women did all the work on the skins, and around every tipi these skins were staked out on the ground to dry. Skins used for clothing and tent covers were tanned to a creamy white, a long and laborious task.

With the food supply readily obtainable, Plains people had more time for sewing and painting, feasting and ceremonies, and interminable warfare over horses. The abundance of buffalo hides and free time permitted a renaissance in painted hide art. Women painted intricate geometric designs on parfleches (storage bags) and rawhide chests, while the men painted naturalistic designs on buffalo robes, tipi covers, and linings. Each tribe as it moved to the plains adopted some of the customs of their predecessors, but also molded them to fit their own life. It was a cultural renaissance that died almost as quickly as it was born.

During this time the horse became the standard of value. A class system grew up based on the number of horses a man owned. A prosperous family had at least a dozen horses to carry their tent, clothing, furnishings, and food, but the average family had only three or four horses so that they overloaded their horses and had to use dogs as well. The poor had to rely on help from others, the loan of horses, and discarded clothing and lodge covers. But the poor always had one avenue out—a poor but ambitious youth could always rise through horse stealing; many of the greatest chiefs started out the poorest. Then again, those rich in horses always stood a chance of becoming paupers overnight by the same process.

The Plains Indian year consisted of four seasons of unequal length. Winter was a five-month season when the camp stayed in one place. Camps were small and spread out along the mountain foothils and river valleys—wherever trees provided shelter and fuel. Spring was a difficult time since the buffalo moved out onto the plains and could not be followed in the snow. This was the time for making tipis, lazy-backs, and other tipi furnishings.

When the buffalo reached prime condition in June, the scattered bands gathered together for the great tribal hunt. The entire tribe assembled in great camp circles and celebrated the Sun Dance and the Renewal of the Sacred Arrows. The Cheyenne camp, of more than a thousand tipis, formed concentric circles three and four deep and a mile in diameter. One camp, seen at the Little Big Horn, numbered two thousand tipis in five concentric circles. Within the camp circle there were several special tipis—those belonging to the chiefs and the large Warrior Society lodge. At the center, a large council lodge was erected from two combined tipis. The camp circles were designed like the tipi itself with an opening, the "door," facing east.

In the fall another great hunt was held. The buffalo meat was now fat and good for pemmican, the Indians' winter survival food. The meat was dried, pounded, mixed with fat and berries, and then stored in rawhide parfleches. With the approach of winter, each band made ready to move to the winter campground. The night before the move, belongings were packed into bags, and lazy-backs and mats were rolled up.

With the first glimmer of dawn camp was struck. In a flash the whole tipi village was flat on the ground. The lodge covers were rolled up and placed on

MOVING

A hole is burned near the end of each lodgepole so that it can be lashed to each side of a packsaddle.

A horse can carry up to a dozen lodgepole. This meant two horses were needed to carry the poles & a third to carry the cover & furnishings. The ends of the poles wore down quickly & a new set of poles might be needed each year.

Dogs originally carried the poles so their length was limited

The lodge cover is always folded in the same way.

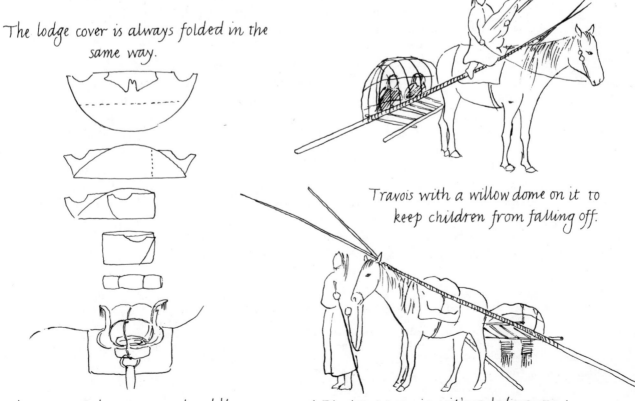

Travois with a willow dome on it to keep children from falling off.

The cover tied onto a packsaddle.

A Blackfoot travois with a lodge cover.

horseback or travois, the poles bundled up and placed on either side on a horse. Scouts rode on ahead and the camp moved out. First came mothers with cradles on their backs followed by horses pulling travois with willow domes containing the young children. Then came the herds of horses driven by the young boys. Where the march encountered deep rivers rafts were made of tipi poles and bull boats were used as ferries. By midafternoon the march was halted. The camp chief chose the campsite and the women picked out the tipi sites. Within an hour every tipi was pitched and a fire was burning in the hearth.

THE TIPI

Everything the Power of the World does is done in a circle. The sky is round, and I have heard that the earth is round like a ball, and so are all the stars . . . Our teepees were round like the nests of birds, and these were always set in a circle, the nation's hoop, a nest of many nests, where the Great Spirit meant for us to hatch our children. But the Waischus have put us in these square boxes. Our power is gone and we are dying, for the power is not in us any more.

—BLACK ELK

The tipi is the most ingenious conical tent ever devised. Under the impetus of nomadic life the Plains Indians invented a frame system that would enable them to pitch a tent quickly. The pole frame was given a pattern that improved the ability of the cone to resist wind and enlarged the spacial arrangement inside. Along with this they devised a ventilation system that freed the interior of smoke, the bane of all other conical tents, and with the addition of a lining they created a warm, draft-free interior space. There are few tents that equal the tipi as a simple-to-construct yet comfortable dwelling.

The first written reports of the tipi are from the Coronado expedition of 1540, which told of villages of buffalo-skin-covered conical tents that were moved by dogs. It appears that most of the essential tipi characteristics existed at this time. We know from the remains of ancient tent rings* that tipis of this era were small, averaging little more than twelve feet in diameter. The tipis of this era were only used part of the time—winters were spent in earth lodges.

Once the horse was introduced, the tipi became larger (the horse could carry the longer poles required of a larger tipi) and its territory expanded. The tipi spread so far because there was always a ready supply of buffalo skins for the cover and because it could be used in just about any terrain or climate. The tipi could take advantage of the sheltering qualities of the environment available at different times of the year. This was particularly important in the winter

---

* Several kinds of tents use stones to weigh down the edges of the covering and hold the tent against the wind or because pegs can't be driven into frozen or rocky ground. When the tent is moved, the stones are rolled back leaving a circle of stones. These "tent rings" often stay in place for centuries and provide valuable clues—and often the only available record—as to tent sizes and settlement patterns. They are found throughout American Indian, Inuit, Siberian, and Lapp countries.

time since the tipi had little insulation of its own. It could be said that the old earth lodge was superior protection from the elements—both cooler in the summer and warmer in the winter—but the tipi could partially overcome this disadvantage by moving into the shelter of the forests in the winter and cool, wind-swept places in the summer.

Each tribe that adopted the tipi changed the design slightly so that any tribe could be identified by its own particular tipi style. The tipis of the Crow had long poles; Chipewyan tipis had smoke flaps made of separate pieces of material; the Cheyenne used long, thin smoke flaps while the Blackfoot made theirs short and fat. For a short period, the Plains was a great design laboratory in which every conceivable variation of this simple conical tent existed.

But almost as soon as it began it was over. The Native Americans were forced onto reservations and discouraged from living in the tipi—since it was a "pagan house." However, photographs of the period invariably show a tipi pitched beside a log house. The tipi was not readily given up, and every summer the people would move out of the hated log houses and into the tipis. But with time, the tipi ceased to be used as a home and was only seen at special occasions and on movie sets. A few Native Americans and a few white converts continued to live in tipis and to keep the knowledge of their construction alive. Reginald and Gladys Laubin (*The Indian Tipi*) collected the essential information on tipi construction and themselves lived in and visited many tipis. In time, the tipi was reconsidered, and there is now a minor renaissance of tipi dwelling. The tipi is being considered for what it is—a simple-to-construct dwelling that can be made as comfortable as any shelter Western man has imported to this land. There are now at least three companies in this country manufacturing tipi covers, linings, and poles.

THE SIBLEY TENT

It is ironic that the troops sent out to conquer the tipi-dwelling peoples and force them to give up their "pagan houses" lived in the Sibley tent. This tent, and the stove that went with it, were invented by General Sibley for use in the Plains wars and were based on tipi design. The tent had low cylindrical walls and a conical roof through which protruded a stove pipe—basically a tipi adapted for use with a stove—and it proved to be superior to those tents in use by the U. S. Army at the time. It might be said that the tipi dwellers' own tent aided in their defeat.

TIPI CONSTRUCTION

There are two essential characteristics that distinguish the tipi from other conical tents: It is not a true cone (it tilts backward), and it has smoke flaps. Pre-Columbian tipis possessed these features, but the horse nomads improved and refined these attributes as they increased the overall size of the dwelling. The backward tilt produces several advantages: It braces the tipi against the wind; it increases the usable interior space; and it permits the hearth to be moved forward of center, which permits head clearance in the rear of the tent.

But without doubt the greatest of the tipi innovations is the ventilation system—the tipi is the only conical tent that does not become smoke filled when there is a fire inside it. The main device for clearing the interior of smoke is the smoke flaps which channel the wind in such a way as to draw the smoke out of the tipi. The smoke flaps are attached to poles so that they can be adjusted according to wind direction. When the wind is directly behind the tent, the flaps are held pointing away from the wind. With a head-on wind, the flaps can be turned sideways, and in case of rain or snow they can be folded over each other to close the smoke hole.

Interior ventilation is also aided by the addition of a lining or "dew cloth," a piece of material that hangs from the tent poles and runs around the interior of the tent. The dew cloth insulates the interior, prevents drafts, and keeps out rain that runs down the poles. It is tied to the pole at the top while the bottom is turned in—sealing out wind that blows under the cover. The dew cloth is often painted with bright geometric designs.

THE FRAME

The feature that distinguishes one conical tent from another is the arrangement of the frame poles—all North American conical tents use simple straight poles for the frame. These poles are the most consistently patterned in the tipi frame, and the "patterns" always start with a three- or four-pole foundation. The Laubins make a strong claim that the three-pole foundation is more rigid than the quadrapod, and that with only three poles used for the foundation, more poles can be grouped in the front of the tipi. But this is really a question of individual preference and style. A map of the Plains shows a distribution with the western tribes favoring the three-pole and the eastern tribes favoring the four-pole foundation. In addition, each tribe had its own particular tie at the apex of the foundation and its own particular placement of poles in the foundation.

The length and number of lodgepoles determines the diameter of the tipi. Before the horse, the average tipi was twelve feet in diameter and used fifteen foot poles. The average horse nomad family had a tipi of eighteen or twenty feet in diameter and used poles twenty-one to twenty-five feet long. Occasionally tipis were made quite large—thirty to fifty feet in diameter—but these tents were difficult to move and so were rare. The poles generally projected from three to six feet above the apex. The Crow tipi poles were made so long that the tent looked like an hourglass.

FRAME

The frame begins with a foundation of three or four poles lashed at a point that equals the radius of the cover.

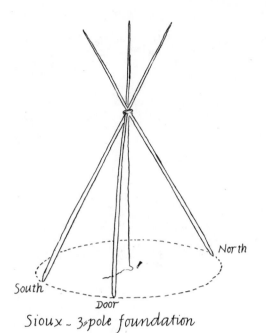

Sioux – 3-pole foundation

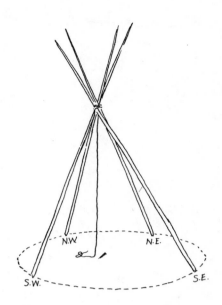

Blackfoot 4-pole foundation.

Each tipi has a characteristic configuration of poles at the apex. This is a 3-pole Cheyenne.

A 4-pole Crow tipi from the front.

After the foundation is set up, the rest of the poles are added. The anchor rope is wound four times around the apex & pulled down & tied to a peg at the center.

COVER

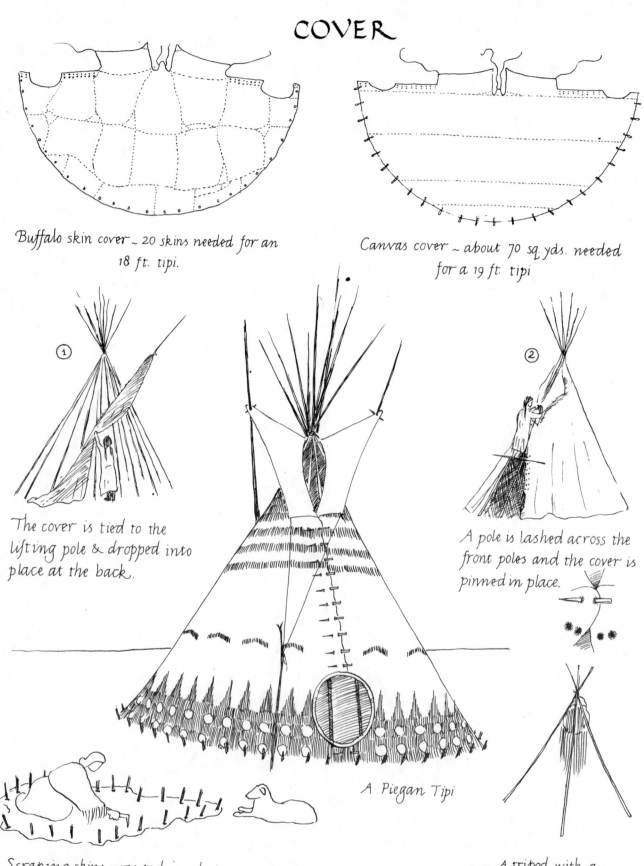

Buffalo skin cover ~ 20 skins needed for an 18 ft. tipi.

Canvas cover ~ about 70 sq. yds. needed for a 19 ft. tipi

① The cover is tied to the lifting pole & dropped into place at the back.

② A pole is lashed across the front poles and the cover is pinned in place.

A Piegan Tipi

Scraping skins was tedious but necessary work.

A tripod with a medicine bundle hanging from it.

TIPI ENGINEERING

wind → The tilt of the tipi braces it against the prevailing winds. This also permits the fire to be moved forward of center which gives more room in the rear.

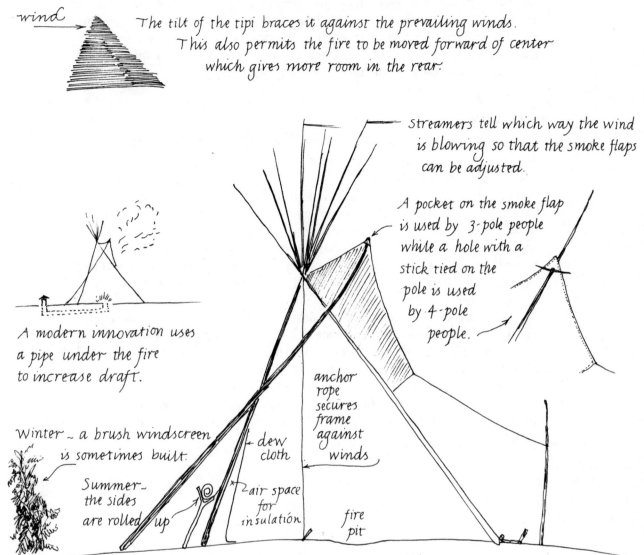

Streamers tell which way the wind is blowing so that the smoke flaps can be adjusted.

A pocket on the smoke flap is used by 3-pole people while a hole with a stick tied on the pole is used by 4-pole people.

A modern innovation uses a pipe under the fire to increase draft.

Winter – a brush windscreen is sometimes built.

Summer – the sides are rolled up.

dew cloth

air space for insulation

anchor rope secures frame against winds

fire pit

Tipis are pitched on high spots if possible so that it is unnecessary to dig a trench.

DOORS

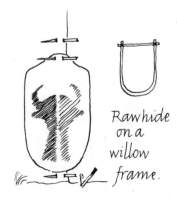

Rawhide on a willow frame.

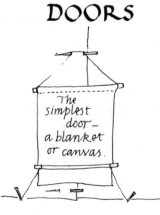

The simplest door – a blanket or canvas.

Canvas on a willow frame.

Men always cut and trimmed the lodgepoles. The preferred wood was lodgepole pine which was plentiful in the foothills of the Rockies where the tribes camped. In other places cedar, spruce, tamarack, or white pine was used. A good set of lodgepoles was a valuable possession—five poles were equal in value to a horse. The poles had to be replaced every other year as they wore down from the dragging. Each pole weighed about twenty pounds so that a horse could drag about eight or ten poles lashed to either side of it.

THE COVER

The women of the house owned the tipi and did the most work in its construction. Women did all the work on the lodge cover. A woman who wanted a tipi collected many buffalo hides, then tanned them, and scraped them thin to reduce weight and let more light into the tipi. Summer hides were preferred because they were thinner than winter ones. A small twelve-foot tipi required eight to ten hides, a fourteen-to-sixteen-foot tipi used twelve to fourteen hides, and an eighteen-foot lodge used twenty-two hides. When enough hides were tanned, a great feast was held and all the participants sewed the skins together under the direction of an older women. The sewing was done with bone awls and sinew thread.

The finished cover was hoisted onto the frame and closed up. A smudge fire was built inside and the cover thoroughly smoked to make it water repellant and keep it pliable after a rain. The completed lodge was then dedicated, and all were invited to a large feast to demonstrate the generosity of the owners. As the buffalo disappeared, canvas covers began to replace skin covers. These had the advantages of lightness and required less sewing, but nothing will ever replace the beauty of the soft white buffalo-skin cover painted in designs of earth colors.

Men painted the designs on the tipi and the lining. Only a few tipis were painted—those of the specially honored and the medicine men. The designs—which confer supernatural powers to the tent dweller—were painted according to instructions received in a dream. The owner of the tipi went to a painter and told him her dream. The artist made the outlines with a buffalo-tail brush and

directed others as to where to fill in the colors. The bottom band was usually red, symbolizing earth. The area above this—the sky—was painted with white discs, symbolizing stars. At the top, a black band indicated the night sky with circles for the Great Bear and the Pleides.

The lodge cover lasted only a year or two. Old covers were given to the poor who trimmed off the rotten bottom edge and used the cover on their smaller tents. Among some tribes the dead were left untouched in the tipi—the tent was allowed to die with its owner.

An older woman always directed the placement of the tents in the camp. Her sharp eyes picked out the high spots so that in case of rain the tipi floor would stay dry. The tipi was always pitched with the door facing east so that when the sun came up in the morning one could give thanks to it. This also kept the door opposite the prevailing westerly winds and the frame properly tilted against the wind. Winter camps were set in river valleys or sheltered wooded

Inside the tipi – the dew cloth is painted with geometric designs. Willow back rests are set in place. The couple sit on a buffalo robe. A rawhide chest sits by the wall.

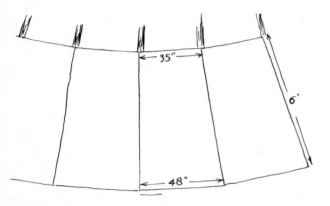

The dew cloth (lining) keeps water running down the poles out, prevents drafts & the air space in back of it helps to carry the smoke upward & thus clears the air.

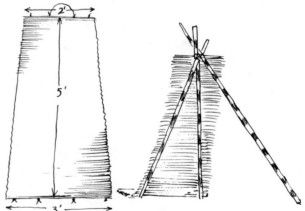

Willow back rests (lazy-backs) are made by threading willow rods on sinew. It is held up by a tripod of poles. The whole can be rolled up to move.

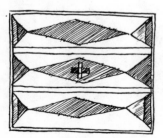

Parfleche design

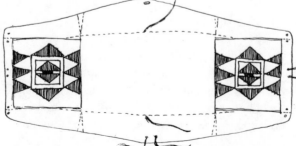

The parfleche is made of a single piece of rawhide & painted with geometric designs.

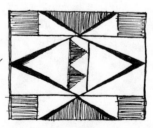

Parfleche design

spots with brush walls built around the tipi as a snow and wind fence. Summer camps were placed in higher areas to take advantage of cooling winds.

PITCHING THE LODGE

The tipi frame can be set up in five minutes, and the cover attached and pinned in fifteen. The foundation is set up with the help of an anchor rope which one person holds back while another places poles in position. The anchor rope is wound around the apex of the crossed poles and down and around the tent to the anchor peg. The cover is put in place with a lifting pole from the back. A pole or two lashed across the door poles serves as a ladder so that the cover can be pinned down the front. The edge of the cover is pegged down; a stone maul is used to drive the pegs (the same maul is used to break bones and firewood and pound pemmican). In high winds, stones are placed on the edges.

The interior arrangement of the tipi should be familiar by now—it is encountered in the Mongolian yurt, the Lapp kata, the Siberian conical tents as well as the tipi. In spite of the great distance and many centuries separating the earliest conical tents of Asia from the lordly tipis of America, these things have remained the same: the conical shape, the central hearth, the two sacred areas, and the place of honor between them. Although these tents differ widely in construction and materials and are spread over half the globe, they have retained what must be very ancient beliefs about the nature of a dwelling and how it should be ordered for the benefit of man and the gods. There is something magical about sitting in a circle around a fire: The hearth fire becomes the hub of the tent, the tent dwellers the spokes of a sacred wheel.

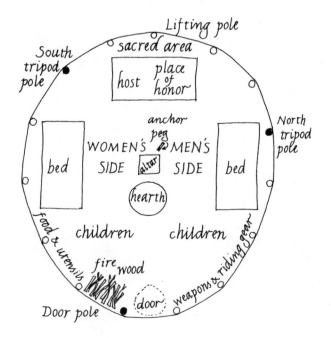

SOURCES

My primary sources for this book were ethnographies, travel books, and *National Geographic* magazine. The most imporant source was *La Tente Noire* by C. G. Feilberg—my guide through all of the confusing material I found along the way. It not only covers the black tent, but most other nomad tents as well, and its bibliography is inexhaustive. The Bedouin tent and its North African relatives are minutely described and illustrated in Rackow and Caskel's *Das Beduinenzelt*. Andrews has a detailed description of the Moor tent. Edelberg, Ferdinand, and Dupree cover current knowledge of the Persian black tents. Nicolaisen's work on the Tuareg is a complete study of the material culture of a mat-and-skin tent people. Anyone investigating the yurt must start the Kharuzin. Siberian tents are detailed by Jochelson and Levin and Potapov. For information on the tents of the circumpolar zone, Birket-Smith (1929) has a chart of material culture elements for the area and a complete bibliography. Koerte offers a good survey of Canadian native shelter. The tipi is thoroughly documented in Laubin.

BIBLIOGRAPHY

ADNEY, EDWIN TAPPAN. *The Klondike Stampede.* New York: 1900.

ANDREWS, PETER ALFORD. "Tents of the Tekna, Southwest Morocco," in Paul Oliver, ed., *Shelter in Africa.* New York: 1971.

BARTH, FREDERICK. *Nomads of South Persia.* Boston: 1968.

BIRKET-SMITH, KAJ. *The Caribou Eskimos. Report of the Fifth Thule Expedition,* Vol. 5. Copenhagen: 1929.

————. *Primitive Man and His Ways.* New York: 1957.

BOAS, FRANZ. *The Central Eskimo. Sixth Annual Report, Bureau of American Ethnology.* Washington: 1888.

BOGORAS, VLADIMIR. *The Chukchee. I. Material Culture. Memoir of the American Museum of Natural History,* Vol. 7. New York: 1904.

BRIGGS, LLOYD CABOT. *Tribes of the Sahara.* Cambridge, Mass.: 1960.

BUSHNELL, DAVID. *Native Villages and Village Sites East of the Mississippi. Bureau of American Ethnology.* Bulletin 69. Washington: 1919.

CARPENTER, EDMUND; VARLEY, FREDERICK; and FLAHERTY, ROBERT. *Eskimo.* Toronto: 1959.

CHAPELLE, JEAN. *Nomades noire du Sahara.* Paris: 1958.

CIPRIANI, LIDO. *La Abitazioni Indegeni Dell'Africa Orientale Italiana.* Napoli, Italy: 1938.

COLE, DONALD POWELL. *Nomads of the Nomads, The Al Murrah Bedouin of the Empty Quarter.* Chicago: 1975.

COLLINDER, BJORN. *The Lapps.* Princeton, N.J.: 1949.

COON, CARLETON. *Caravan: The Story of the Middle East.* New York: 1951.

————. *The Hunting Peoples.* Boston: 1971.

COOPER, MERIAN. *Grass.* New York: 1971.

CRONIN, VINCENT. *The Last Migration.* New York: 1957.

DENSMORE, FRANCES. *Chippewa Customs. Bureau of American Ethnology,* Bulletin 86. Washington: 1929.

DOUGHTY, CHARLES M. *Travels in Arabia Deserta.* London: 1921.

DUPREE, LOUIS. *Afghanistan.* Princeton, N.J.: 1973.

EDELBERG, LENNART. "Seasonal Dwellings of Farmers of North-Western Luristan," in *Folk,* Vol. 8. Copenhagen: 1966.

EKVALL, ROBERT B. *Fields on the Hoof, Nexus of Tibetan Nomadic Pastoralism.* New York: 1968.

FEILBERG, C. G. *La Tente Noire.* Copenhagen: 1944.

FERDINAND, KLAUS. "The Baluchistan Barrel-Vaulted Tent and Its Affinities," in *Folk,* Vol. 1. Copenhagen: 1959.

————. "The Baluchistan Barrel-Vaulted Tent," in *Folk,* Vol. 2. Copenhagen: 1960.

GAUDRY, MATHEA. *La Société Femme au Djebel Amour et Ksel.* Alger: 1961.

GIDDINGS, J. L. *Kobuk River People.* College, Alaska: 1961.

GOLVIN, L. *L'Art de la Tente.* Alger: 1960.

INSTAD, HELGE. *Nunamiut; Among Alaska's Inland Eskimos.* New York: 1954.

JOCHELSON, WALDEMAR. *The Koryak. Memoir of the American Museum of Natural History,* Vol. 9. New York: 1908.

———. *The Peoples of Asiatic Russia.* New York: 1928.

———. *The Yakut. Anthropological Papers of the American Museum of Natural History,* Vol. 33. New York: 1933.

JOHNSON, DOUGLAS L. *The Nature of Nomadism. A Comparative Study of Pastoral Migrations in Southern Asia and Northern Africa.* Chicago: 1969.

KENNAN, GEORGE. *Tent Life in Siberia.* New York: 1910.

KHARUZIN (or CHURUSIN), N. *The History of the Development of the Dwellings of the Nomadic and Semi-Nomadic Turkish and Mongol Tribes of Russia* (in Russian). Moscow: 1896.

KOERTE, ARNOLL. *Towards the Design of Shelter Forms in the North. Phase I: Native Shelter Forms.* Winnipeg, 1975.

KRADER, LAWRENCE. *Social Organization of the Mongol-Turkic Pastoral Nomads.* The Hauge: 1963.

KRIST, GUSTAV. *Alone Through the Forbidden Land; Journeys in Disguise Through Soviet Central Asia.* New York: 1938.

LAND, C. "The Admirable Tents of the Shah Savan," in *International Archives of Ethnography,* Vol. L, Pt. 2. 1966.

LAOUST, E. "L'habitation chez les transhumants du Maroc Central I, La tente et le douar." in *Hesperis,* Vol. X. Morocco: 1930.

LAUBIN, REGINALD and GLADYS. *The Indian Tipi.* Norman, Okla.: 1957.

LEECHMAN, DOUGLAS. "Wigwam and Teepee," in *The Beaver.* Winnipeg: December 1944.

———. "Igloo and Tupic," in *The Beaver.* Winnipeg: March 1945.

LEVIN, M. G. and POTAPOV, L. P. *The Peoples of Siberia.* Chicago: 1964.

LEWIS, I. M. "Northern Pastoral Somali of the Horn" in J. L. Gibbs, *People of Africa.* New York: 1965.

LHOTE, HENRI. *Les Touraregs du Hoggar.* Paris: 1944.

LIPS, JULIUS. *The Origin of Things.* New York: 1947.

MANKER, ERNST. *People of the Eight Seasons.* New York: 1963.

MASON, OTIS T. *Women's Share in Primitive Culture.* New York: 1898.

MATHIASSEN, THERKEL. *Material Culture of the Iglulik Eskimos. Report of the Fifth Thule Expedition,* Vol. 6. Copenhagen: 1928.

MCKENNAN, ROBERT A. *The Chandalar Kutchin.* Washington: 1965.

MOWAT, FARLEY. *Canada North.* Boston: 1968.

MURRAY, G. W. *Sons of Ishmael. A Study of the Egyptian Bedouin.* London: 1935.

MUSIL, ALOUIS. *The Manners and Customs of the Rwala Bedouins.* New York: 1928.

NATIONAL GEOGRAPHIC SOCIETY, ed. *Nomads of the World.* Washington: 1971.

NICOLAISEN, JOHANNES. *Ecology and Culture of the Pastoral Tuareg.* Copenhagen: 1963.

NORBU, THUBTEN JIGME and TURNBULL, COLIN M. *Tibet*. New York: 1968.

OSGOOD, CORNELIUS, contrib. *Ethnography of the Kutchin*. New Haven: 1936.

PAULSON, IVAR. "The Seat of Honor in Aboriginal Dwellings of the Circumpolar Zone, With Special Regard to the Indians of North America," in Sol Tax, ed., *Indian Tribes of Aboriginal America*. New York: 1949.

PEHRSON, ROBERT N. *The Social Organization of the Marri Baluch*. Chicago: 1966.

POPOV, A. A. *The Nganasan: The Material Culture of the Targi Samoyeds*. Bloomington, Ind.: 1966.

RACKOW, ERNST and CASKEL, WERNER. *Das Beduinenzelt*. Baessler-Archiv XXI: 1938.

SCHURMANN, H. F. *The Moghols of Afghanistan*. The Hague: 1962.

SHOR, JEAN and FRANC. "We Dwelt in Kashgai Tents," *in National Geographic*. Washington: 1952.

SMITH, E. BALDWIN. *The Dome*. Princeton, N.J.: 1950.

SPECK, FRANK. *Penobscot Man*. Philadelphia: 1940.

TURI, JOHAN. *Turi's Book of Lapland*. New York: n.d.

TURNER, LUCHIEN M. *Ethnology of the Ungava District. 11th Annual Report of the Bureau of American Ethnology*. Washington: 1894.

VERITY, PAUL. "Kababish Nomads of Northern Sudan," in Paul Oliver, ed., *Shelter in Africa*. New York: 1971.